Happenings

HAPPENINGS

Developing Successful Programs
for School Libraries

PATRICIA J. WILSON
ANN C. KIMZEY

1987
LIBRARIES UNLIMITED, INC.
Littleton, Colorado

LIBRARIES UNLIMITED, INC.
P.O. Box 263
Littleton, Colorado 80160-0263

Library of Congress Cataloging-in-Publication Data

Wilson, Patricia J. (Patricia Jane)
    Happenings.

    Bibliography: p. 109
    Includes index.
    1. School libraries--Activity programs. I. Kimzey,
Ann C., 1940-   . II. Title.
Z675.S3W754   1987   027.8'223   87-3190
ISBN 0-87287-522-9

Libraries Unlimited books are bound with Type II nonwoven material that
meets and exceeds National Association of State Textbook Administrators'
Type II nonwoven material specifications Class A through E.

For Wendell and Stephanie
with love
and for Steve who would
have been so pleased.

Contents

Figures

FIGURE

Introduction

Programming for library patrons is certainly not a new concept. Public libraries routinely budget for, plan, and execute programs. What is more unusual, however, is integrating this kind of activity into school libraries. Through our own experience working in libraries and training school librarians we have discovered that little, if any, real programming is structured into school library activities. With this in mind, this book is designed to encourage school librarians at all levels to plan and execute library programs as part of their day-to-day library activities.

The contents of this handbook should provide the librarian with an understanding of the meaning of library programming; assist in the complex process of planning and evaluating a library program; stimulate creativity in identifying topics, ideas, and resources for programs; and provide some sample forms which aid in the entire programming process. The bibliography provides references to resources on audiovisual and print materials which will aid in program development.

We begin with an explanation of library programming and its place within the school library picture. Chapters 2, 3, and 5 address the specifics of programming, which include planning, organization, execution, and follow-up. Chapter 4 contains detailed descriptions of nine programs spanning the grade levels and illustrating a broad spectrum of approaches. When appropriate, illustrations of sample forms appear in the text.

This book draws upon our past experiences as librarians in creating successful school library programs. Our experiences and observations have led us to conclude that library programs can serve as a highly effective means for a school library to meet a variety of educational objectives in unique and unusual ways. Our major objective is to encourage programming and to foster a better understanding among our colleagues of the vast array of possibilities that programming offers. Furthermore, we want to ease and simplify the process of programming to such an extent that most obstacles such as time and budget constraints, which traditionally hamper school librarians, can be circumvented. Indeed, programming can become such an exciting and rewarding part of school library activities that, we hope, the librarian, students, faculty, and even perhaps the administration will insist it be a part of the library schedule. We ask only that you approach the following pages with an open mind and an active imagination. Then give it a try. We feel the results will be both pleasing and beneficial to all.

What It's All About
An Overview of Library Programming

WHAT IS LIBRARY PROGRAMMING?

Library programming is not a new software package for a microcomputer. It is people—students, teachers, parents, community members—involved in interesting activities which produce excitement and enthusiasm for everyone involved. Naturally, the school librarian orchestrates these "happenings." In other words, school library programs consist of planned activities which are organized and executed to fulfill a predetermined set of objectives. Descriptions of library programs will be as varied as those given by the proverbial blind man describing an elephant. While there is no prescribed formula, each program's objectives will shape its form and determine its complexity. Although the activities will vary greatly, all programs will serve to promote the school library or learning resources center.

In this work the terms *library*, *learning resources center*, *media center*, and other variants are used interchangeably, as are *librarian*, *media specialist*, *learning resources specialist*, and other variants. The reader should not infer that there is some subtle difference implied.

RELATED RESEARCH FINDINGS

While there is a wealth of information on public library programs, few references to school library programs appear in the literature. What research is available, however, indicates that students' use of libraries and their attitudes towards libraries and librarians can be affected in a number of ways.[1] Librarians must extrapolate from this research when designing library programs, and creatively incorporate proven techniques as well as introducing experimental activities. Just which techniques and activities are chosen will depend upon the objectives for any given program. Some valid objectives include:

- To increase student awareness of the existence of the library and its staff, facilities, and services.

- To counteract any perceived stereotyping of the role of the librarian or of the library.

- To promote positive relations between teachers and library staff.

- To supplement classroom curriculum materials.

- To promote the enjoyment of reading and foster reading as a recreational activity.

RATIONALES FOR LIBRARY PROGRAMMING

Awareness of Library/Learning Resources Centers

Programming promotes recognition of specific aspects of the library such as its staff, resources, facilities, and services. This is especially valuable in schools with large student bodies and faculty. Regardless of the size of the school, in order to serve a purpose the library must be recognized and understood, even if this recognition is as simple as knowledge of the librarian's name and role.

Consider a high school with an enrollment of 2,500 students, many with no study hall period, thirty-minute lunch periods, and five-minute breaks to change classes. Perhaps, the students have one English class during which they are to spend the hour in the library (along with three biology and science classes which are scheduled to be there at the same time). Will these students be able to identify which adult is the librarian? If not, how can a student possibly ask the librarian for help?

Or consider an open house or parents' night at an elementary school. Parents have assembled to meet the teacher, but how many hurry to the library to meet the librarian? How many even stop to consider if there is a library or librarian? If parents think about the library at all, it is probably to assume it exists and is adequate to meet the students' needs. Although there are exceptions to these attitudes, they are truly the exceptions to the general rule.

These two vignettes proclaim the same message: **Promote yourself!** Be a pro-active librarian. Programming is an excellent way to accomplish this. In fact, an entire program may be designed around the objective of making others aware of the school library.

Curriculum Support

Consider the curriculum design for the school and also the materials needed to support the subject matter.[2] Anticipate the subjects that will be emphasized and plan a program to highlight the library's resources in that area. If the library is somewhat short on the necessary resources, expand the program to direct students to outside supplementary resources.[3] Be sure to ascertain in advance that the outside resources are available and exist in sufficient levels and numbers to meet the student demand.

Community and Public Relations

Programming can link the school library to the general community. Everyone in the community supports the school through taxes, not just the parents of students. When developing a community resource file (see chapter 3), take a few moments to consider the possibility of incorporating some of these resources into a library program. A focal point could be a popular local event such as an annual Future Farmers of America (FFA) livestock show or a special feature of the locale (either natural or man-made). This type of program can feature related materials from the learning resources center, local experts, and appropriate activities outside the library. Remember that while this type of programming promotes aware-ness of all these resources, the community becomes aware of the school library and its role in the educational process. There is the additional possi-bility of attracting media coverage and extending the recognition process beyond the local area.

These suggestions are certainly not in any way intended to present an exhaustive treatment of rationales for including programming in school library activities. Each program should begin with a specific objective or set of objectives. The rationales presented here are only representative in nature.

TYPES OF PROGRAMS

Programs take shape in a wide variety of types. This is to say, the librarian is limited only by his or her own creativity and physical endurance. Chapter 4 provides detailed specifics regarding programs. At this point we are addressing only generic types.

Programming for Target Groups

Programs might focus on special target groups within the population of the library's general users. The target group might be as large as the entire student body or as small as the members of the computer club or drama club. A program does not have to offer something for everyone but rather should focus on specific objectives which should implicitly or explicitly identify the population for which the program is intended. An excellent way for those who are nervous about programming and have limited space, resources, or time, to get started is to plan the first program for a small target group. However, the daring type can try something on a larger scale.

Programming with Focus on a
Specific Theme

Another approach to developing a program involves focusing on a particular theme. Again, specific objectives must be clarified and related clearly to the theme, specifying how the theme supports or relates to the objectives. The theme might be a serious one (e.g., drug addiction, teenage pregnancy, latch-key children, crisis help). Juxtaposed to the serious themes are the more lighthearted topics: crafts and hobbies, pets and pet care, space exploration, careers and career choices, local activities (e.g., the circus, a performance by the Blue Angels, or a local water skiing tournament), and special holidays. It does not matter which comes first, the target group selection or the program content. It depends on the direction one's creative juices start to flow. Chapter 2, which deals with planning a program, will help focus your ideas and thus provide directions for proceeding in an organized fashion.

Programming for Curriculum Needs

Another generic type of programming is that related to school curriculum. Planned in concert with the faculty to make everyone's job easier, these programs can use a learning center or self-administered approach (see chapter 2). Materials would be easily accessible. Special bibliographies could be prepared in advance, and any necessary specialized library skills taught. Then simply announce the opening date. Just include whatever is needed to meet specific objectives.

Programming for Fun

Do not overlook the possibility of planning a program that will be simply enjoyable for those who participate. While there is nothing wrong with this concept, keep a good perspective when designing a program for fun, remembering that it should not detract from the primary responsibilities of the library and librarian. It must be planned in addition to, not instead of, the primary functions of the learning resources center. Also, to ensure its success, be sure your definition of fun is in agreement with the target group. The primary objective in pleasure programming is to entertain those who participate.

Programming for School/Community Relations

Focusing a program on positive aspects within the local community can promote favorable school/community relations. Such a program may be able to foster greater communication between the school population and the members of the community. Careful planning should ensure that no one will be offended and greater concern for local schools and education will be enhanced. The library's community resource file (see chapter 3) will provide a wealth of ideas for this particular type of programming.

Joint or Cooperative Programs

One last suggestion is to consider joint programming. Think about available needs, resources, physical facilities, and users, then take a look around and see if a neighborhood library or other school library might benefit from the same program. Formulate a general outline of the program and then approach the library with the idea. By sharing the work, it might be possible to put together a program that neither unit alone could have managed. If the school libraries in a district are willing, a traveling program might be developed in which the work could be shared, and the audience participation maximized.

LIBRARIAN/TEACHER BOND

Many school librarians feel they work in a vacuum, or at least in semi-isolation. Memos about important curriculum meetings seldom make their way into the library mail box. Students arrive at the direction of a teacher requesting material the library has never owned or has never received a request to purchase. After five years in a large school, a teacher admits not knowing which of the people working in the library is the librarian and which is the clerical assistant. Principals feel that the librarian does not have much to do and can easily handle a spill over group of study hall students. Programming can help resolve some of the misunderstandings between the librarian and other members of the faculty. Library activities become more visible to those not familiar with the "librarian as master teacher" concept.

Programming can foster and develop support and feedback which will enhance future activities. Teachers and students alike will begin to use the resources available to them through the library or learning resources center and the result will be positive for the entire teaching/learning process. Certainly there will be setbacks. The bond you seek to nurture will take time to develop and one program will not do the job. If teacher participation in the program is voluntary, pressure from students will occasionally bring teachers who have initially chosen not to participate to the library door. View this as an opportunity to begin developing relationships rather than an annoyance. Accommodate late arrivals as much as possible as there is nothing to lose and much to gain in many cases.

FACULTY INVOLVEMENT

Once the bond between the faculty and librarian has been forged, or perhaps during the bonding process, make every effort to entice teachers to participate in the programming efforts. Attend grade level meetings and curriculum planning sessions. Invite teachers to meetings and seek their input on potential programs. Have ideas ready to contribute in order to act as a catalyst. However, when teachers begin to offer suggestions, sit back and let the brainstorming process take over. Incorporate ideas offered by faculty whenever possible. Include teachers in the actual programming to the extent they are willing. Acknowledge your appreciation for their ideas, assistance, and support.

The librarian is a master-teacher, and programming allows pro-active involvement as a partner in the education process.

NOTES

[1]Ron Blazek, *Influencing Students toward Media Center Use* (Chicago: American Library Association, 1975); Isabel Schon, et al., "The Effects of a Special School Library Program on Elementary Students' Library Use and Attitudes," *School Library Media Quarterly* 12 (Spring 1984): 227-31; Yvonne A. Hodges, et al., "High School Students' Attitudes towards the Media Program—What Makes the Difference?" (Paper presented at the annual meeting of the Association for Educational Communications and Technology, Research and Theory Division held in Dallas, Tex., 1982; available from ERIC Clearinghouse on Information Resources, Syracuse, N.Y., 1982).

[2]Norman Steinaker, "Ten Years Hence: The Curriculum Development and Usage Center," *Educational Leadership* 33 (March 1976): 447-49; Beatrice E. Angus, *Appraisal of the New York State School Library System* (Syracuse, N.Y.: ERIC Clearinghouse on Information Resources, 1980).

[3]Angus, *Appraisal of the New York State School Library System*; Shirley L. Aaron, *School/Public Library Cooperation: A State of the Art Review* (Syracuse, N.Y.: ERIC Clearinghouse on Information Resources, 1980).

Getting Started
Organizing and Planning a School Library Program

Through effective organization and planning, librarians greatly increase the likelihood of providing students with successful and exciting library programs. Regardless of the size or type of library program under consideration, librarians should begin planning the program several months in advance. By considering the following suggestions, program planners can often avoid the usual pitfall of jumping into program development without preparing adequately for what is to come.

SELECTING A THEME

Where to begin is usually the first question asked when contemplating a special library event. The first step involves the selection of an appealing and appropriate topic or theme. At the same time, librarians should develop programs around topics with readily available resources. For example, a program focusing upon sailing may prove unfeasible for librarians in certain areas where the resource materials and people are not likely to be within easy reach. Why complicate the situation by choosing a program topic which may prove difficult to put together? Therefore, select a topic around which a program can be easily developed.

Student Interests

Student interests offer a primary starting point for possible program topics for without them a program wouldn't get off the ground. Librarians may determine these interests by asking the students and teachers for help. A suggestion box, along with suggestion forms (see figure 1), placed in a centralized location of the library encourages student and teacher input into book ordering as well as program development. By maintaining a record of these suggestions, the librarian can build a list of possible program themes for future consideration. Additionally, student interest surveys (see figure 2, page 12), given to students at the beginning of the school year, offer librarians and classroom teachers some indication of interests at particular grade levels. Librarians can usually divide the questionnaire input into two major categories: fad interests and more permanent interests. While certain fads such as the latest rock and sports stars may come and go, these ephemeral interests should not be overlooked when choosing a program topic. In the second category, we find those topics which interest students of particular grade levels regardless of the generation. These more permanent interests may vary according to age and grade levels within the school. Remembering that the state or area in which the school is located often has an effect upon interests, librarians can easily pinpoint successful program topics. For example, interest in certain sports such as snow skiing or sailing might be greatly influenced by accessibility to the sports. Programs focusing upon the more stable areas of interests can be repeated in the future, becoming more refined with each presentation.

SUGGESTION FORM

_____ We need more books on the following topics:

_____

_____

_____ Please order the following title(s) for our school
library:

_____

_____

_____ We need more books written by the following
author(s):

_____

_____

_____ I'd enjoy attending a program in the library about
the following topic(s):

_____

_____

Fig. 1. Student/teacher suggestion form.

STUDENT INTEREST SURVEY

Grade _____   Sex   M   F

What is your favorite hobby?_____

What is your favorite sport? _____

What types of books do you enjoy reading?

_____ poetry	_____ fantasy
_____ hobby	_____ biographies
_____ sports/recreation	_____ mysteries
_____ animals	_____ realistic fiction
_____ science fiction	_____ historical fiction
_____ romance	_____ science
_____ history	_____ geography

What types of library programs would you enjoy attending?

_____ Travel	_____ Hobbies
_____ Sports	_____ Dance, Music
_____ Art	_____ Careers
_____ Crafts	_____ Cooking
_____ Cultures	_____ Computers

About what specific topic(s) would you enjoy a library program?

_____

_____

Fig. 2. Student interest survey.

School Curriculum

The school curriculum provides stimulus to librarians for generating program ideas. More and more school administrators are realizing the benefits reaped from including the school librarian in curriculum planning sessions. While teachers benefit from the librarian's expertise concerning the available supplementary materials related to the curriculum, the librarian also derives many benefits from the shared planning session. By meeting with specific grade levels or departments, the librarian becomes more cognizant of what goes on at each grade level and the special curriculum needs of the students. In turn, this enables the librarian to better meet the needs of the curriculum through more informed book, audiovisual, and program topic selection. Through curriculum sharing, the entire school community enjoys a well-informed librarian who can use the information gained at planning meetings to enrich and supplement the curriculum. If necessary take a gentle but firm pro-active stance to ensure inclusion in curriculum meetings.

Community Events and Everyday Situations

Librarians often generate program ideas from "happenings" within the community. For instance, a celebration of a local festival or holiday such as Cinco de Mayo Day could present the school librarian with an ideal topic around which to develop a program. Special community events such as a local arts and crafts festival can offer a springboard for a good school library topic. Often the interest for such an event has already been generated by local publicity. At the same time, by focusing upon the topic at school, the community event gains more significance. In this way, programs tied to community events provide an opportunity to foster and promote good public relations between the school and community.

Professional Literature, Conferences, and Workshops

Librarians may also turn to professional literature, conferences, and workshops as possible sources for program topics and ideas. By the same token, professional organization meetings sometimes focus upon activities that have proved successful in the school setting. Learning from the successes and mistakes of others often saves much time in the long run. A special file for topic ideas derived from meetings and clipped from journals comes in handy when trying to decide upon a theme for an upcoming program. With this information at their fingertips, librarians can more easily put together a successful program.

Resource Persons and Materials

The simplest way to select a theme is by matching the student needs and interests to the readily available resources. By calling upon the community resource file (described fully in chapter 3) for this information, a special program topic can usually be quickly and easily decided upon.

SETTING OBJECTIVES

Clear, relevant program objectives form a firm foundation for a successful program. During the early planning stages the librarian must define the objectives of the program. All too often, librarians and teachers haphazardly jump into a program without any real objectives in mind. Early in program development, consider the reasons for presenting the program and the desired end results. The formulation of objectives begins here. These objectives should be based upon the current curriculum needs and interests of the students. Additionally, when establishing these objectives, consider the materials and resources within easy reach. State the goals as clearly and simply as possible, using language that is specific and direct. After defining the objectives, the program planner will find it much easier to determine the format and materials which best suit the program. In the end, these objectives should be measurable in some way for purposes of evaluation. Figure 3 presents examples of program objectives that can offer a starting point.

Finally, always write the objectives down. Some librarians find it quite helpful to lay out their program plans in a manner similar to lesson plans — listing objectives, materials needed, procedures, methodology, method of evaluation, and follow-up activities. Appendix A provides a sample program plan.

Theme: Rodeo Roundup Time

Objectives:

1. To acquaint students with materials in the library which provide information about the central topic.

2. To emphasize the historical background of events which comprise the rodeo activities (e.g., cutting horse event, calf roping).

3. To highlight current activities within the community which are featured at rodeo time (e.g., improvement of stock through breeding and healthcare).

4. To introduce the students to the various skills involved in livestock showing.

5. To share with students the behind-the-scene activities which go on during a rodeo.

Fig. 3. Program objectives.

CHOOSING A FORMAT

Library programs can assume a great variety of formats. These formats will often determine the amount of time and work required of the librarian in order to accomplish the program's desired objectives. Before tackling any program, first evaluate the various formats and carefully select the one which best suits the predetermined instructional goals. Formats can range from the simple exhibit within a display case to a complex learning center, or from an audiovisual presentation to a live production complete with speakers, guest artists, or performers.

Exhibits

An exhibit is one of the least complex formats for library programming. Time spent arranging the exhibits, however, can vary according to the type of exhibit selected. A variety of types exist: the display case, freestanding exhibits, mobiles, wall displays, table displays, or any combination of the aforementioned. The type selected often depends upon instructional objectives and the available physical facilities.

By arranging the exhibits in the school library, librarians often attract students to the library who would otherwise never set foot in the door. For example, a seventh-grader seldom checked out books from the library. Last spring, however, when Indian artifacts were on exhibit in the library, he apprehensively entered the library to view the display. Today this eighth grader regularly enters the library to "see what's happening." Sometimes, in a case such as this, exhibits advertise to students that libraries supply a variety of marvelous educational experiences. Students come to view the library as more than a depository from which to check out books.

Particularly in planning your first program, you may choose to use a display case (or cases), which are reasonably easy to set up. These exhibits, preferably in locked cases, may focus upon a variety of topics. Alone, they may offer a complete program. Alternately, displays may supplement a more complex program which utilizes a mixture of formats. When planning an exhibit for the library, please be sure to keep the following pointers in mind:

- Avoid advertising a particular commercial or industrial company. For example, many local businesses would enjoy exhibiting information regarding their products or services. Such exhibits may create problems within the school library. Once you display specific brands or feature services of a specific company, it becomes difficult to refuse other companies equal time. Strive to keep such exhibits generic rather than brand-name specific. If this is impossible, use a variety of brands in the display.

- Stay clear of controversial topics unless prepared to include material from every point of view. One high school librarian made the mistake of exhibiting a well-prepared display on the generation of electricity using nuclear power. A local community group which lobbied and regularly demonstrated against the generation of nuclear power demanded that the library offer equal time to the antinuclear power position.

- Always consider the security of the items used in the displays. The locked display case provides one possible solution. Try to obtain a waiver of responsibility from any individual or company which provides material used in the display. This problem of protection may cause some librarians to think carefully about this particular form of presentation. Awareness of potential problems is most important.

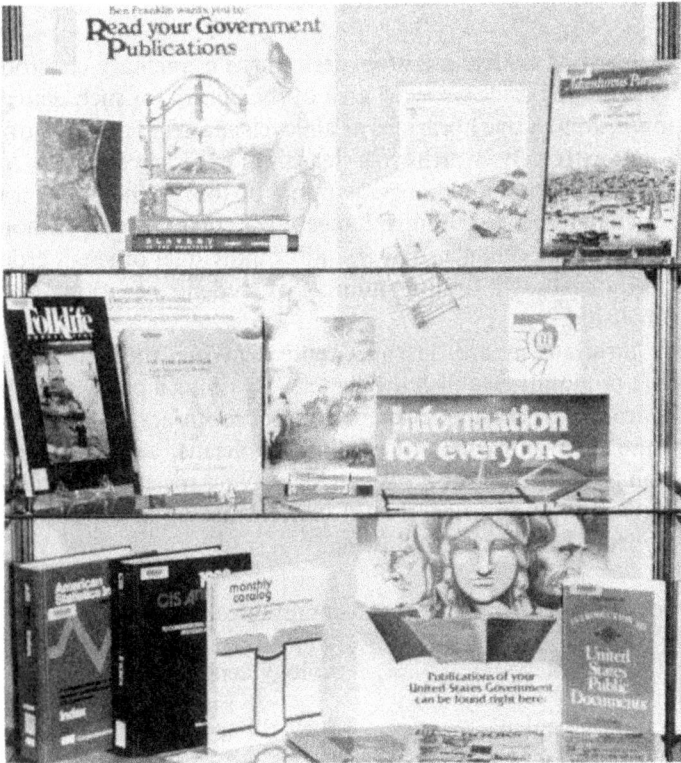

Material from the government documents collections is featured in this attractive arrangement.

Featured Speakers

Try planning a program with a guest speaker as the focal point. Speakers can be most effective in enticing students to participate in library programming. Those willing and able to spend some time in dialogue with the students create a good atmosphere. Even more exciting, encourage the speaker to include illustrations, demonstrations, or audience participation whenever appropriate. Topics can be curriculum related or may focus on special interests of the student body. The speaker need not be among the rich and famous. Your community is filled with untapped potential. The most difficult task is identifying these resources and convincing your selected speaker that he or she has something of value and interest to offer.

Learning Centers

While learning centers are often seen in the elementary classroom, the possibility of setting aside a special area of the library for such centers tends to be ignored. Innovative librarians at all levels may find this type of library program an extremely worthwhile learning experience. Since learning centers can focus upon an enormous range of topics, they offer a unique way of enriching the curriculum and meeting students' needs. Although the format of a learning center usually requires individual or small group participation, librarians will find the number of students benefiting from such centers surprising.

Some librarians sponsor learning center activities throughout the year, while others randomly establish the centers. By filling a particular area with exciting learning experiences related to specific library skills, curriculum needs, or the sheer enjoyment of reading, librarians can give students one more reason to enter the library. When identifying specific activities for the learning centers, the librarian should concentrate upon topics which will interest students, such as the following:

cooking center	communications center
flying center	ecology center
cultural center	storytelling center
crafts center	travel center
computer center	fantasy center
career center	gardening center
music center	farming center
mystery center	art center
author center	library skills center
illustrator center	architectural center
sports center	interior design center
energy center	detective center
environmental center	pet center (fish, birds, hamsters, etc.)
government center	

Some programs lend themselves quite naturally to the learning center format. The centers may be located on a table top, on a bulletin board, in a carrel, or perhaps in a decorated carton that once contained a refrigerator or dishwasher. Other librarians choose to use audiovisual materials in their learning centers. For example, in Lois Ryan's library you'll usually find a center for viewing filmstrips which feature special children's books. Lois always makes certain that her center contains specific instructions for operating the cassette-filmstrip viewer.

Taking a slightly different approach, consider these learning centers as interest centers. Now select from a much broader range of topics upon which to focus. Simply choose an interesting topic, such as rice farming, and arrange an informative display. Then involve the students in the display through various activities. Ruth Parker, an elementary librarian in Louisiana, was born and raised on a rice farm. Using her background knowledge, Ruth planted rice in a large tray and displayed it, along with miniature farming equipment, in a corner designated as the "Rice Farming Center." Colorful posters and photographs illustrating the various stages of rice farming proved informative to the youngsters who eagerly observed the sprouting rice crop.

Demonstrations

Students find demonstrations fascinating, particularly when the demonstrations allow for audience involvement. Librarians who routinely present demonstration activities in the library find enthusiastic and receptive audiences. Cultural activities such as dance, music, or painting are just a few examples of sources for interesting demonstration programs. Generally, the library provides an appropriate setting for the activities, but other locations within the school should be considered if the program requires special physical facilities. For example, a demonstration of the proper use of fire extinguishers would have to take place on the school grounds, but it should be part of the Fire Prevention Week activities.

IDENTIFYING RESOURCES

After determining the topic and formulating the objectives for the upcoming library event, the librarian should identify the available resources which meet the program objectives and needs. To make programming easier, librarians should be encouraged to continuously identify available resources throughout the year. By keeping a record of these resources, as discussed in chapter 3, librarians will have a wide range of resources at their fingertips when starting to plan a library program.

Community Resources

When identifying possible program resources, the community offers a good starting point. Each community, regardless of size, is filled with interesting resources which can add to any library program. These community resources may encompass people, places, institutions, businesses, cultural groups, and organizations within the local community which can supplement or enrich a school program. For example, a library program may focus upon several parents from the school who are willing to share their knowledge of computers with the students. In some cases local businesses may be eager to send employees to speak at your school program. Various persons in the community who are eager to share stories with the students may also be discovered.

By organizing these resources into a centralized community resource file (see chapter 3), librarians and teachers will find program development

Docents from the local symphony association pique students' interests. Reproduced with permission of the Clear Creek Independent School District, League City, Texas.

much simpler. A community resource file serves as a well-organized and readily available source for information relating to persons and materials which can enhance your library program. Chapter 3 offers step-by-step instructions for establishing a community resource file and identifying the available community resources. In addition to assisting the librarian with library program development, such a file can aid classroom teachers in locating a speaker on a particular subject, or provide the teachers with possible ideas for field trips. Sometimes these resources will spark a desire in students for further study or investigation related to the topic.

Librarians will benefit from examining other school and public library community resource files. For instance, by checking the community resource file at the local public library one school librarian located information concerning persons in the local area who collected miniature objects. With this information, the librarian arranged a fascinating exhibit for her middle school library.

Audiovisual Resources

A wide range of audiovisual materials, such as films, filmstrips, tapes, videotapes, and slides can support library programs. In the search for more interesting programs, call upon the audiovisual software available from the library's own collection or consider borrowing these materials from other libraries.

Before deciding whether to use the audiovisual material for a special happening, preview the software to determine whether it meets the instructional objectives and enhances the program. At times, librarians and teachers incorporate a movie or filmstrip into a program, and the software may add little to the presentation. Evaluate the software prior to using it, and determine whether it enhances the program.

Occasionally, librarians develop an entire program around a specific piece of software. For short programs tied to the curriculum, this is a relatively easy way to build a program. Realizing that the eighth grade was studying about Kenya, one enthusiastic middle school librarian developed an entire program on Kenya around a commercially produced slide/tape, presentation. While highlighting the mutual benefits gained by teacher/librarian planning, this example also emphasizes the relative ease of planning a program around a special and worthwhile audiovisual production.

How do we identify the appropriate audiovisual materials for a particular program? Various selection tools (see appendix B) are readily available to help librarians in selecting audiovisual software for their collections. While often arranged according to topic, such selection tools help in matching audiovisual materials to specific topics. Further checking to determine cost and availability of selections will be needed.

Some businesses and institutions publish catalogs that inform librarians and teachers of the various audiovisual software they have available, either free of charge or for a fee. Such sources can supplement a planned program. Librarians often discover that renting a particular piece of audiovisual software is a bargain, particularly when an item will be used only one time. Again, be certain to evaluate the software prior to the program.

Some guidelines to aid in identifying the appropriate audiovisual software include:

- Will the audiovisual material enhance the planned program?

- Is compatible equipment readily available?

- Does the format of the audiovisual software enhance the program through its ease of use, or does the format detract from the program?

- Will the audiovisual material appeal to the students identified as the target group? (Consider the topic and length of presentation.)

- Will all students be able to easily view the audiovisual presentation?

Exhibits and Displays

When highlighting a particular topic, library programmers sometimes turn to the various types of exhibits described earlier: display cases, bulletin boards, wall displays, free-standing displays, mobiles, and table exhibits. Identification and selection of exhibits involves knowledge of the various private individuals and the commercial organizations which can provide libraries with exhibits. While these sources vary in cost from free to expensive, they do make library programming simpler. By including these exhibit resources in a community resource file, the task of identifying exhibit sources becomes much easier.

Often students provide an untapped source for a wide variety of displays. After tiring of empty display cases, both in the library and in the hallway approach to the library, Stephanie Williams decided to begin a program entitled "Entertaining Diversions." All the boys and girls in the school were encouraged to complete a questionnaire describing special hobbies and interests. From these questionnaires, a student library display committee selected particular topics to highlight each month. The students did most of the work, with only some assistance from the librarian. The displays ranged in subject from hobbies to travel to special interests.

Interest center attracts young readers. Focus attention on certain materials by grouping them in a special interest center. Reproduced with permission of the Clear Creek Independent School District, League City, Texas.

Hobbies offer an outstanding source for exhibits. Stamp collecting, coin collecting, and shell collecting are only some good topics to highlight in the library. Special hobbies or collections belonging to parents, teachers, and students within the school appear to be one of the most readily available sources for exhibits. While some exhibits may simply involve arranging interesting items focusing upon a particular theme in a library display case, others can become more involved. The questionnaire described in chapter 3 for determining community resources enables the librarian to pinpoint local sources for such exhibits.

Many organizations prepare and distribute preconstructed exhibits. Covering a wide range of subjects, these displays can easily be correlated with the school's curriculum and materials already available in the library. (Consult both chapter 3 and the bibliography for resources for such exhibits.) This type of display may carry a rental fee, but often the fee will prove minimal. Such exhibits provide the librarian with one of the least time-consuming means of programming. Simply advertise the event, set up the exhibit, and relax and enjoy the enthusiasm it generates.

Student artwork and projects provide librarians with other great sources for exhibit material. Teachers and students are always quite happy to share their work with others by putting it on exhibit. Special projects to share in the library may include student-made stories, artwork, book reports, and special research projects. Librarians may choose to display the student work on bulletin boards, library walls, shelves, or tables. One elementary librarian, Paul Jackson, selected a special wall and designated it as the "student gallery." Each grade level was asked to select a specific month during which the students and teachers in that grade were responsible for providing the gallery exhibit in the library. Paul Jackson, with the help of parent volunteers, arranged the exhibit materials. Posters scattered throughout the school announced the gallery showing for the month and invited everyone to come and enjoy it. By displaying these creations in the library, the pupils developed a sense of pride in and value of their hard work.

The most obvious source for displays is books themselves. The best way to call attention to library materials is to display them. Selection of the books for display may depend upon a librarian's needs. New books can be displayed in a special area labeled "New Arrivals," or students can be attracted to seldom-circulated material through a creative presentation of these underused items. Books on display will have a much higher check out rate, so plan accordingly. Be prepared to relinquish the book and have a replacement for it under the counter.

Adolescent and Children's Literature

When considering possibilities for library programs, librarians should not overlook the wealth of adolescent and children's literature. Besides exhibiting books, programs may focus upon books by a particular author, or they may highlight books on a specific topic.

Particular literary works related to the program topic can easily be identified by using the subject cards of the card catalog file. The librarian may also choose to integrate community resources or audiovisual materials into these programs which highlight literature. While focusing upon Rudyard Kipling as the program topic, Ann Doland used a commercially produced filmstrip, book exhibits, and displays of student research projects to develop an entire library program.

Other outstanding programs which focus upon literature may include a visit by a local author or illustrator of children's books. If such a visit cannot be arranged, consider teleconferencing as an alternative. By arranging an author or illustrator interview through a conference telephone call, the librarian acquaints students with a particular author or illustrator. Chapter 4 provides a detailed look at a program focusing upon teleconferencing.

Learning Centers

Identification of learning center activities should be based upon student interests as well as curriculum needs. Too often librarians assume that programs must be based only on curriculum needs, and they fail to recognize the importance of selecting material based upon student interests. Once the user's attention has been gained, other programs which are more tightly focused on learning needs will also be appealing.

Occasionally the interests and/or hobbies of a librarian will provide a stimulus for a special program. One of the best programs using a learning center approach developed from Susan Adams's interest in tropical fish. Several large aquariums, donated by parents whose children had tired of the time and care required to maintain them, were placed in various parts of the library. Pamphlets, books, catalogs, and reference material about fish placed in each center provided participants with needed information. Bright, attractive, graphically illustrated posters from the local fish store drew attention as students entered the room. The aquariums attracted so much attention that the teachers began using these centers as part of their science units. After the students learned the basic requirements to maintain each aquarium, various classes assumed the responsibility on a specific schedule. The interest level will eventually drop, but the financial investment caused no budget strain, and the aquariums may serve a future purpose. Librarians should consider their own interests and background knowledge when selecting possible learning center themes.

Regular Storytime

A regularly scheduled storytime in the media center increases the programming possibilities for the elementary level. This special twenty- to thirty-minute period each day or on selected days of the week can take place without hampering the librarian's schedule. Chapter 4 provides a detailed program at the elementary level which focuses upon storytime.

When identifying the resources for this type of program, librarians must first look for volunteers willing to share stories with the youngsters. Detailed information concerning how to locate these persons is in chapter 3. The questionnaire (see figure 9, page 46) sent to parents for the purpose of establishing the community resource file provides an easy source for identifying possible storytellers. Parent volunteers usually delight in reading aloud or telling stories for this special event. Very special persons such as the school principal will definitely attract eager listeners. One special resource which librarians often overlook is grandparents living with students, who often have a variety of stories which they look forward to sharing with youngsters.

When identifying the particular stories to share with the students, the librarian may encourage input from the storytime volunteers. The volunteer reading or telling the story usually does a better job if he or she is very familiar with the work. The librarian's own knowledge of literature and student preferences provides the expertise needed in identifying specific stories for storytime. The librarian could also encourage students and teachers to suggest specific stories.

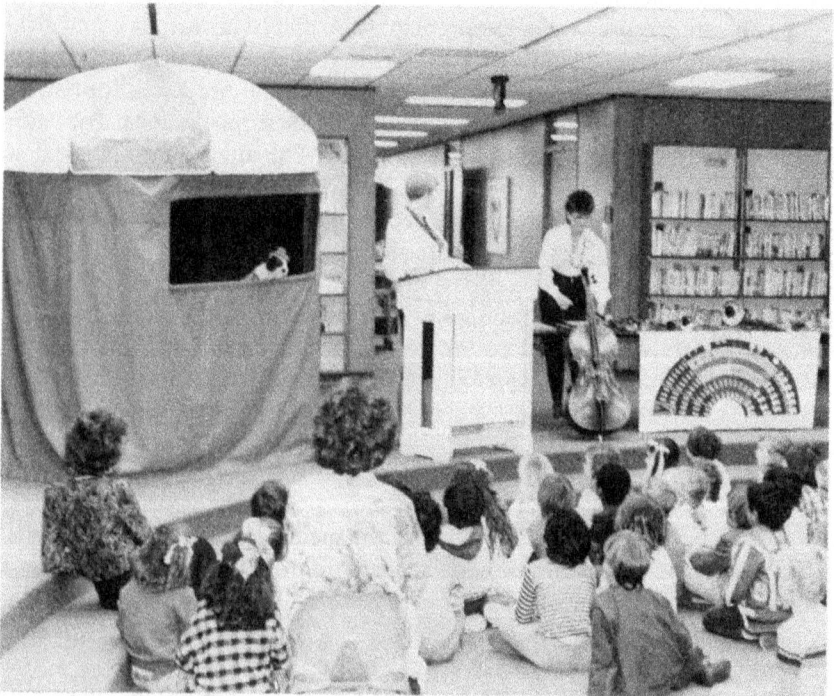

Community resources share their knowledge and stories with students. Reproduced with permission of the Clear Creek Independent School District, League City, Texas.

Special Community Events

School librarians can often tie community events to a library program. Newspaper and magazine articles as well as television and radio announcements often identify these special events taking place in the community. Librarians can often develop an interesting program by using themes and topics based upon a special community event. An additional benefit to the library and school will occur if the library activities share in media coverage of the community event.

MATCHING AUDIENCE TO APPROPRIATE TOPIC

One creative middle school librarian chose romance novels as the topic for a special spring program. The audience receptiveness to the program fell short of the librarian's expectations. After evaluating the program, she realized that the topic was not suited for an audience of both boys and girls. Had the librarian thought out the program more fully, she would have realized this prior to the program.

Before scheduling any type of program the librarian should properly evaluate the resource according to these guidelines:

- Is the topic appropriate for the age of the audience?

- Can the topic hold the audience's attention?

- Can the planned activities hold the audience's attention?

- Is the length of the activity appropriate for the particular audience?

- Is sufficient new knowledge gained from the use of the particular resource or supplemental activity?

In other words, the program developer must match the topic and the program activities to the special needs and interests of the anticipated audience. By doing so, each program becomes a unique learning experience which satisfies the student's special needs.

OBTAINING PERMISSION FROM
SCHOOL ADMINISTRATORS

Many school districts require that teachers and librarians receive permission from the administration before involving students in a planned program. Even if your district does not make this requirement, librarians and teachers usually benefit from sharing upcoming programs with administrators. Librarians should aim for a good rapport with the school principal and administrators, and discussing program plans with them is a good way to start. In addition, librarians may receive beneficial input from the administrators. The usual hierarchy for permission to proceed with a program varies according to the school district policies. While many school districts require approval only from the principal, other districts expect librarians to receive permission from authorities at a higher level. At the same time, some school districts require written permission, and others need only verbal agreement. Any information, regardless of the rules, extended to school administrators and school board members concerning programming results in better relations between the librarian and the administration. This atmosphere of positive relations may very well prove helpful at a later date when requesting funds for the library.

IDENTIFYING DATE AND TIME

Early in the planning stages the librarian must give special consideration to the selection of the date and time. Confirmation of this date and time, however, should be at a later point when more information concerning the program is available. Identification of date and time is no easy matter. In determining the date and time, the librarian must consider three important factors: availability of speakers/participants on a particular day, the school calendar, and availability of backup resources such as volunteers and audiovisual software.

First, the program planner must discuss convenient times and dates with the people involved in the program. Often these people must arrange their volunteer time according to their heavy work schedules. In the earliest planning stages, program planners should request two or three possible dates on which these people could take part in the library program.

Knowledge of the school calendar warrants careful attention when planning any program. Watch for other scheduling conflicts, making certain that no other special events have been planned for that particular date. In addition, knowledge of lunch and class change schedules of your target group is an important consideration. Teachers do not appreciate changes in their students' schedules, and good rapport with the teachers is the single most important ingredient for successful programming. Talk over the time and date with the faculty well in advance of the program, and invite suggestions. In the outcome, teacher approval of the time and date should increase the chances of the students' enthusiastic support for the program.

Many program planners tend to leave the scheduling of support material and support persons for library programs until the last minute. In identifying the time and date, however, the availability of the materials (software, audiovisual equipment, exhibits) and volunteers who will support the program should be considered. Such volunteers may help seat the children, operate the audiovisual equipment, or supervise the library during the program. No program can run smoothly without consideration of these important volunteers during the early phases of planning.

IDENTIFYING THE LOCATION

The media center, a natural setting for any library program, can offer an extension to the classroom environment. Offering programs within the library setting encourages library usage by those students who rarely enter the library on their own. Through such programs these nonlibrary users come to view the library as more than a place to check out books. They soon perceive the school library as a gathering place for exciting educational events. While viewing this learning environment as a place filled with important happenings — exhibits, special speakers, and nonprint materials — these students come to see the library as a fascinating hub in the educational process. Above all, the library becomes a place that offers a variety of experiences for everyone.

Occasionally, the librarian may decide that the program should occur in an area outside the library. After all, there is no strict rule that library programming must take place within the library setting. Perhaps, due to the nature of a certain program, the librarian may decide to move the program outdoors. A successful library program in a New Mexico high school highlighted hot air ballooning. The arrival and presentation by a local balloonist required that the program take place on the school grounds. Librarians may choose to locate certain program activities in other areas of the school. Consider the hallways, cafeteria corners, or patio areas when selecting a location for a special program. A successful program sponsored by a New York middle school library focused upon a local ballet group. Since the program required a great deal of open space, the librarian arranged the program setting in the auditorium.

Field trips, sponsored by the library, may also take the particular target group away from the usual library setting. A visit to a publishing company or to the public library may prove interesting programs. In such cases, the school rules and provisions for field trips must be carefully followed.

SELECTING PARTICIPANTS
AND/OR MATERIALS

Preparation for the event must begin well in advance of the scheduled date. Contact the individuals selected to participate at least one month prior to the big event, and first discuss with them needs and objectives. Try to get a feeling as to whether the person will appeal to the intended age group and will meet objectives. Unless these two criteria are satisfied, it would be desirable to rethink the project at this point. Some modifications would definitely be in order.

Once it has been determined that the person meets these criteria, find times and dates mutually convenient for the program. Be certain to inform the participants about the size and age of the audience and what the audience will expect to gain. At this time, talk over the length of the program. Determine if the person or exhibit calls for any special equipment, handouts, or technical needs. Emphasize the necessity of sticking with the date and time at this point. Often people who are not involved in an educational setting are totally unaware of the difficulties encountered by having to reschedule.

One week prior to the program, again contact the individual, business, or exhibitor, for a final reminder of the date, time, and location of the event. Additionally, a simple written reminder proves helpful in many instances. Make the person fully aware of the necessity of being on time, as the success of this kind of event depends heavily upon adhering to all preset scheduling.

CONTINGENCY PLANS

After deciding upon a date and time convenient both with the person and the school schedule, always consider an alternate date that is mutually acceptable in case unusual and/or unforeseen circumstances should arise. Anticipate as many problems as possible prior to the program and prepare appropriate contingency plans to deal with them if they should occur. Unfortunately, the old axiom, "If something can go wrong, it probably will," can be all too accurate when dealing with programming. It should be made clear to the participant that the librarian will need to know about any problems in advance. It is difficult to explain a change of plans to a group of expectant and excited students.

Always be prepared for the unexpected. Librarians experienced in programming recognize the importance of considering alternate speakers related to a particular topic in case the original person cancels out completely. This always ensures a successful and smooth-running program regardless of weather, illness, and other problems.

PUBLICIZING THE EVENT

The previously mentioned high school librarian in New Mexico attributes the success of the hot air ballooning program to the publicity of the event by the students. The entire school seemed to get caught up in ballooning. Students made papier-mâché balloons and posters advertising the event. The school newspaper department contacted the local newspaper concerning the "happening."

Publicity for the upcoming event must begin two to three weeks prior to the occasion in order to build enthusiasm among the students. At the same time, this publicity enhances the image of the media center. After identifying the students involved in the program—perhaps the entire student body or a particular grade level or class—begin to involve students from that group in the program. Encourage them to take part in the publicity process by making and hanging posters to advertise the event. In this way more and more students become a part of the program before it ever takes place, thus ensuring successful response. To further whet the students' appetites announce and describe the upcoming program during classes in the library. Student-made invitations to school administrators and parents as well as student newsletters offer other means by which the students can participate in publicizing and preparing for the event. Intercom announcements also remind the students and teachers of the intended program, date, and time.

The success of any program, however, depends heavily upon the classroom teachers. Enthusiasm on the part of a classroom teacher will rub off on the students and means more than any amount of formal publicity. Without such support and enthusiasm the most carefully planned programs can fail. This is why it is essential that program ideas be shared with teachers and their input be sought in the very earliest planning stages. No program is successful without teacher enthusiasm.

Through publicizing the programs, both before and after they happen, the students' parents become aware of the exciting events which take place in the library. Such positive school experiences offer excellent opportunities to increase good public relations between the school and community. Be certain to contact the local newspapers, radio stations, and television stations concerning special programs (see figure 4, page 32). The public needs to focus upon the innovative "happenings" within the schools. Unfortunately, the media often spotlight the negative news. Try to change this by making local news sources aware of the positive events. Additionally, through such media coverage the public becomes more aware of ways to contribute to the educational process within the schools. Otherwise, these special events go unnoticed by the public.

SAMPLE NEWS RELEASE

MIDDLEBROOK ELEMENTARY SCHOOL
1222 South Street
Anytown, Anystate 99999

FOR IMMEDIATE RELEASE

CONTACT

June Koller, Librarian
Middlebrook Elementary
433-8558

The students of Middlebrook Elementary enjoyed a treat last Tuesday (Feb. 12). The local jazz dance troup, Razzamataz, gave three performances to an enthusiastic audience. Students are studying dances of various cultures. This performance was the highlight of a week-long program, featuring motion picture and video tapes of a wide variety of dance styles. To conclude the study program, the students will learn and perform special dances at Parents Night on Monday, February 25. All community residents are cordially invited to come and enjoy this event.

Fig. 4. Sample news release.

Another benefit which can result from publicity includes teaching the students the various aspects involved in advertising. Perhaps, advertising and marketing professionals from the community may share the procedures related to this important aspect of any business with the students. In this way, the students can experience a hands-on part in publicizing the impending library program.

SCHEDULING CLASSES

The scheduling of classes so students can attend the event tends to be the most intricate and time-consuming task related to program preparation. Scheduling takes much time and planning by the librarian and depends upon the cooperation of the classroom teacher. For all programs it is important to talk to teachers in advance and to give them a chance to give some input into the scheduling of the event. When organizing the simplest of library programs, the librarian can make arrangements for all classes or particular target groups to attend the event at one scheduled time if there is sufficient seating space. Therefore, certain programs in which various classes attend the program at different times involves a more difficult scheduling procedure. The librarian must consider many details such as other special events scheduled at that time, physical education and music schedules, lunch schedules, and class changes. This often makes scheduling much more difficult; however, a good rapport with teachers often leads to their developing a more congenial attitude toward the librarian's scheduling problems. Teachers tend to be more flexible if they support a particular program and have had some say in the program planning.

Gentle reminders as to the library program time and the schedule for various classes can be posted in the teachers' lounge area and sent to classrooms on the day before the program to reinforce the idea of being on time. When scheduling small groups to come at alternate times, a student or volunteer to remind the next class of their time proves helpful. In such an ongoing program, timing of arrivals and departures is an essential factor for the success of the program.

PREPARING STUDENT AND PARENT VOLUNTEERS

Without the help of student and parent volunteers, few programs can take place. Call upon these volunteers early in the program planning. Assign them special tasks in order to make the program run smoothly. Make certain all volunteers know what their job entails. The tasks of arranging furniture, operating audiovisual equipment, reminding classrooms of assigned times to arrive in the library, monitoring traffic flow, and greeting guests can be assigned to volunteers. This takes some of the pressure off of the librarian. Chapter 3 offers detailed information concerning volunteers.

Thanks to Parent Teacher Association (P.T.A.) volunteers, dressed as clowns, a Circus Day program in a small elementary library in Texas ran smoothly. During the program, the students visited with three people stationed in the library who discussed behind the scenes events at the circus. The most crucial element of the program was the traffic flow. As the students moved to the various stations in the program, the P.T.A. clowns escorted the students.

ARRANGING THE FACILITY

Arrangement of Furniture and Seating

Librarians must consider carefully the furniture and seating arrangements compatible with the type of program planned. Questions to take into consideration include:

- Will the children sit in chairs or on the floor?

- Does the speaker have any special needs regarding seating arrangements or speaker podium?

- Where will the speaker stand?

- Will the speaker need amplification to be heard?

- Where will the librarian sit?

- Will grade levels sit together?

- Will the shorter children be able to see the program?

- Where will the teachers sit?

- Where will the guests sit?

- Does seating for the participants need to be provided?

- Where should the furniture be placed?

- Who will help arrange the furniture?

Begin to arrange the furniture and seating on the day prior to the program. Because help may need to be enlisted if larger pieces of furniture are involved, it may be necessary to enlist the support of student or parent volunteers. Always keep in mind the importance of completing as many tasks as possible prior to the program day. This gives the librarian more time to visit with participants and take care of unexpected problems. Again, always try to anticipate possible problems and prepare for them in advance.

Arrangement of
Displays and Decorations

Attractive displays and decorations will add to the learning environment. If at all possible, arrange displays and decorations the day prior to the event. Decorations, ranging from balloons to models and book displays, offer easy ways to make the event more festive. Students usually enjoy taking part in this preparation, and their involvement in setting up displays and decorating creates additional enthusiasm over the program. Additionally, banners and posters made by students can enhance the programs.

Providing Audiovisual Equipment

Keep in mind the general flow of the program and be sure that audiovisual materials will enhance the presentation. Keep in mind the following suggestions for using audiovisual materials:

1. Preview the audiovisual software to determine its appropriateness. Study any available guides. Decide if the audiovisual material actually enhances the program. If it adds little to the program, don't use it as it will waste valuable time. Feel comfortable with the equipment or make certain the person using it will be at ease with the equipment.

2. Prepare the environment. Prior to the program arrange the facility for viewing. Check the lighting and temperature. The audience should be able to see the screen without any problem. Make certain the audiovisual equipment is working properly. Set up and load the audiovisual equipment ahead of time so it will be ready to go. Always have backup equipment and bulbs at hand. Plan for the worst. If the program participant is showing the software, make certain he/she feels comfortable with the equipment.

3. Prepare the audience. Give the students possible questions to consider while viewing the software. Always share the program's objectives for showing the audiovisual material with the students.

4. Give the students a chance to interact with the program whenever possible. The audiovisual equipment may be stopped at a key point and questions may be asked.

5. Encourage follow-up activities. These may simply include a follow-up discussion concerning the audiovisual program. Then again, the follow-up activities may involve actual activities resulting from the audiovisual production.

6. Evaluate the program. Be prepared to make modifications in a repeat presentation based upon what happens in steps 1-5.

Librarians must make arrangements for special audiovisual equipment in advance. Consider the following questions several days prior to the program:

• What equipment do the participants need?

• Will the participants provide their own equipment?

• Is the equipment in good working order?

• Where should the equipment be located?

• Are back-up equipment and extra bulbs available and handy?

• Do the participants need a podium or a table and chair?

• Will the equipment need to be moved during the program?

• What software is needed?

• Do the participants need a chalkboard or a chart stand?

• Are extension cords needed?

• Do the participants need someone to run the equipment?

• Who will take care of the lighting?

If possible, set this equipment up in its proper location the day prior to the program. Try out the equipment to make certain it is in good working order. Check the focus and sound level as well as quality of projection under prevailing lighting conditions.

Prior to the program the librarian should make sure the guests feel comfortable with the equipment. Often the guest may request that someone else operates the equipment. In this case, the librarian may take over the task, or better yet, may assign this responsibility to a student. Always allow plenty of time for the student to practice using the equipment, and be certain to familiarize the student with the proper techniques for operating the specific equipment.

PROVISIONS FOR TRAFFIC FLOW

Programs which involve only a few classes will not create major traffic flow problems. However, for the larger programs which involve the entire school, the librarian must make arrangements for the traffic flow several days prior to the program. Questions to consider and discuss with the faculty include:

- In what order will the classes arrive?

- At what point do the classes enter?

- Are a sufficient number of volunteers or student helpers available to help supervise the traffic flow?

- How much time is needed to get all students to the area designated for the program?

- In what order will the students depart?

- Do particular classes have any special problems such as handicapped students which must be considered in advance?

- Do classes or individual students have any special needs such as leaving early?

Model programs in chapter 4 provide specific examples of how librarians deal with the problem of traffic flow.

DAY OF THE PROGRAM

After making most of the program arrangements a day in advance, the librarian can enjoy greeting the guest or guests. A final checklist for this important day may include:

- Check seating arrangements.

- Check audiovisual arrangements.

- Remind teachers and students of the program time.

- Check temperature, lighting, and ventilation.

- Make certain the guests realize the importance of sticking to the schedule.

- Inform guests that you will subtly motion to them when their time is up.

- If possible take your guests to lunch.

- Following the program, allow some time to spend with the guests.

CONCLUSION

If at this point planning a program seems far too time consuming and too much additional work, remember, the rewards are worth far more than the cost in time and effort. Remember, too, that programs can be set up in all sizes. For a first attempt, think small. Use the program checklist in figure 5 to help organize your thoughts. Limit the participants, limit the length of the program, limit the number of activities, but do try it! Both the model programs and program ideas described in chapter 4 will provide a springboard from which to launch your first efforts.

PROGRAM CHECKLIST

Several Months Prior to Event
_____ Decide upon theme/topic
_____ Develop objectives
_____ Identify available resources

One Month Prior to Event
_____ Obtain permission from administration
_____ Select participants
_____ Select materials
_____ Identify audience, date, and time
_____ Contact participants
_____ Begin publicizing event

Develop contingency plans:
_____ Alternate dates
_____ Alternate activities
_____ Alternate speakers

One to Two Weeks Prior to Event
_____ Schedule volunteers
_____ Determine seating arrangements
_____ Determine traffic flow
_____ Give teachers schedule of event
_____ At faculty meeting, discuss event (problems, schedules, etc.)

Day Prior to Event
_____ Prepare seating arrangement
_____ Prepare audiovisual equipment
_____ Prepare decorations, displays, exhibits
_____ Remind volunteers and participants of time
_____ Remind teachers of schedules

Day of Event

Last minute check of facility:
_____ Room temperature
_____ Lighting
_____ Room arrangement
_____ Audiovisual equipment and cords
_____ Speaker podium
_____ Seating arrangement
_____ Inform volunteers of duties
_____ Greet speakers

After the Event
_____ Do informal evaluation
_____ Do formal evaluation
_____ Send letters of appreciation to participants
_____ Analyze program

Fig. 5. Program checklist.

3

People, Places, and Things
Resources for Library Programs

After organizing and producing a library program plan, the next step is locating the resources for the program. Each community has a wealth of resources, but exactly how does the librarian go about locating those which are appropriate for library programs? Community resources include people, places, businesses, organizations, and institutions within the community which can enrich and supplement the school curriculum. These resources are far too valuable to be overlooked, as is often the case. By taking time to become familiar with, and organize these resources for future reference, librarians will find a wide variety of program ideas readily available at their fingertips. After surveying the community for potential resources, librarians should organize these ideas into a special community resource file.

COMMUNITY RESOURCE FILE

When developing a community resource file, first decide upon the most suitable format for your library's needs. Some librarians prefer a folder format. The folders, filed alphabetically by topic in a filing cabinet, allow space for the community resource information form (see figure 6), as well as pamphlets and any additional handouts related to the resource. A more commonly used and simpler format consists of recording the information concerning each resource on cards which may be filed in a card catalog (see figure 7, page 44). Some librarians find that using a slightly larger card format, for example a 4-by-6-inch format, provides space for more detailed information. Cards this size will not fit into the standard card catalog, but can be placed in a file box. If either the folder or 4-by-6-inch format is chosen over the regular card catalog format, reference cards can be separately filed in a standard card catalog to supplement the community resources catalog (see figure 8, page 45).

Regardless of the format chosen, record detailed information concerning each community resource which has been contacted. Include the following items:

- Name of person, business, company, institution.

- Address and phone number.

- Time available.

- Length of program.

- Special audiovisual equipment needs.

- Target group.

- Fees.

- General program description.

After arranging this information in the order which best suits your needs, be certain to note the date on which the card or folder enters the file. This date will prove helpful in the future when updating your file. Many librarians choose to arrange these cards or folders alphabetically by topic of program. If appropriate, provide a cross-reference to the name of the individuals or companies as well.

By making the community resource file easy to use and by placing it in a convenient location, librarians will find that it can become more than a source for library programs. Soon teachers will be using it for program ideas and field trip information for their own classrooms.

SAMPLE COMMUNITY RESOURCE
FORM FOR FILE FOLDER

TOPIC

NAME _____

CONTACT PERSON_____

Address _____

_____

Phone   _____

TYPE OF PROGRAM _____

GRADE LEVELS _____

LENGTH OF TIME REQUIRED   _____

EQUIPMENT NEEDS _____

AVAILABILITY _____

FEES_____

PROGRAM DESCRIPTION _____

_____

_____

_____

_____

Comments & Additional Information _____

_____

_____

Fig. 6. Sample community resource form for file folder.

TOPIC

Name: _____   Phone: _____

Contact Person: _____   Grade Levels: _____

Address: _____   Fees: _____

_____   Type of Program: _____

Availability: _____   Length of Time Required: _____

Scheduling: _____   Special Equipment Needs: _____

_____

Program Description:

Comments & Additional Information:

Date _____

Fig. 7. Sample card for community resource file.

CAREERS

See also

COMMUNITY RESOURCE FILE

O

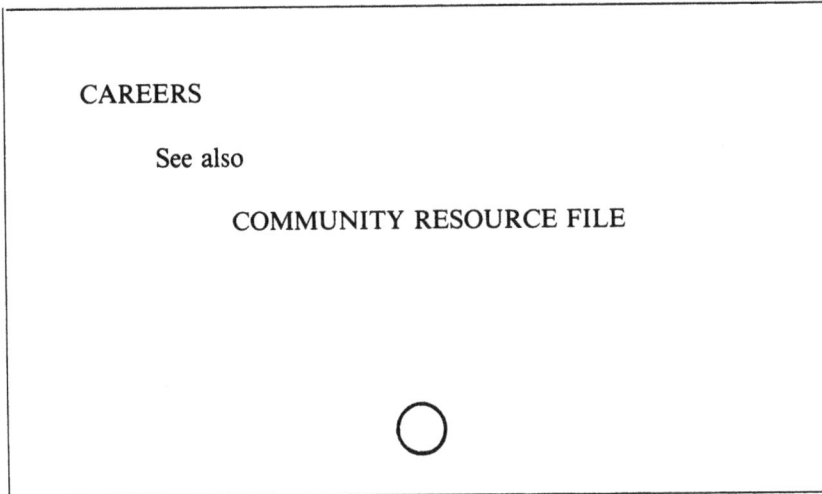

Fig. 8. Sample catalog card reference to community resource file.

IDENTIFYING COMMUNITY RESOURCES

Begin searching for community resources by devising a plan. Make a general outline of the types of community resources which relate to school curriculum and needs. This outline will expand once the search begins. Particular means of identifying the community resources will be discussed in this section.

Questionnaire

Before beginning to search the community for interesting resources, consider the resources within your own school. With the help of a simple questionnaire, interesting talents, skills, and hobbies which the students' parents and grandparents possess can be easily identified. After developing a questionnaire similar to the one found in figure 9, page 46, people who have slides or photographs of special travel experiences can also be identified. Specific information which should be on the form includes: unique talents, special skills, interesting collections or hobbies, and travel experiences which the parent would enjoy sharing with the students within the school. Those parents interested in sharing their interests with the

Dear Parents:

　　To further enrich your child's curriculum, our school library is planning various programs for this school year. Perhaps you have a special talent, interest, hobby, or craft you would like to share with the children at Johnson Elementary. Please complete the following questionnaire if you would like to participate in one of our exciting library or classroom programs. Return the questionnaire to your child's teacher.

Thank you,

Pat Ellis, School Librarian

- -

Date _____

COMMUNITY RESOURCES QUESTIONNAIRE

_____ Yes, I would like to share information/materials with the children at Johnson Elementary.

Name_____　　Phone_____

Name(s) of Child(ren)　　　　　　Name(s) of Teacher(s)

_____　　_____

_____　　_____

Special Hobbies/Crafts:

　　Description of Hobby/Craft: _____

　　_____

　　_____ I would be willing to discuss it with students.
　　_____ I would be willing to demonstrate it.
　　_____ I would be willing to share it with children as an exhibit.

Special Talents/Skills:

　　Description of Talent/Skill: _____

　　_____

　　_____ I would be willing to discuss it with students.
　　_____ I would be willing to demonstrate it.
　　_____ I would be willing to share it with children as an exhibit.
　　_____ I would like to share my storytelling ability with the students.

Travel Experiences:

　　Description (places): _____

　　_____ I would be willing to discuss it with students.
　　_____ I have slides, films, or photographs to share with children.
　　_____ I have interesting materials from this country to share with children.

Fig. 9. Community resources questionnaire.

students should complete the form and return it to the school library. These parents can be outstanding choices when a program need arises.

Before sending the questionnaire home with the students, be certain to receive permission from the principal. Occasionally, principals are not eager to involve parents in school programs. If this occurs, arrange a time to discuss the library's objectives and explain in some detail how the information will contribute to the educational process. Be diplomatic but persistent. Show the principal some examples which illustrate the potential benefits of such data.

Yellow Pages of the Telephone Directory

A wide assortment of resources within the local community can be located by using the Yellow Pages of the telephone book. Simply examine the Yellow Pages and decide which companies, businesses, institutions, and organizations could provide exciting program possibilities.

Before contacting anyone, develop a format arrangement for the community resource card (see figure 10, page 48). Plan ahead, and decide which questions to ask the resource person. A librarian who is well-organized with questioning will find that the telephone interview will take very little time. Begin the conversation by introducing yourself and school. Give the person some idea about the nature of your call. It is a pleasant surprise to find out how willing people and businesses within the community are eager to cooperate. Many companies and businesses as well as institutions have established public relations departments, which is where the librarian should start. Some companies consider sending speakers to local schools an important part of their public relations with the community. Students can play an important role in the advertising process for these businesses.

After giving the potential resource person some background information concerning the library's needs, the following questions may be asked:

- Would you be interested in sharing information concerning your field of expertise with the students?

- Where are you located?

- Is your company, business, etc., willing to send persons to the school?

- Is there any fee involved?

Topic _____   Date _____

Name _____   Grade Level _____

Address _____   Availability _____

_____   Equipment
Needs _____

Phone _____   Fee _____

Description:

Comments:

- The *date* you add the card to the file is necessary to help you keep the file up to date.

- The *topic* includes the subject area, hobby, career, etc., upon which the resource focuses. The file cards are usually filed alphabetically by topic.

- *Grade level* includes the target group most appropriate for the presentation.

- *Availability* includes the days or times the resource person is available.

- *Equipment needs* includes any special audiovisual needs.

- *Description* includes general information on the type of presentation one may expect.

- *Comments* may include information concerning the responses to the particular program.

Fig. 10. Sample card for community resource file.

- What do you have to offer students?

- To what age students do you feel your material will relate?

- Will you need audiovisual equipment?

- What is the length of time needed for the program?

- Are there certain days when you are available?

- How much notice do you require?

- Will you supply any handouts for the students?

- What other services are available?

- What will be the general content of your presentation?

After the telephone interview the librarian must decide whether to enter the person or organization in the community resource file. To determine this, consider the curricular needs of the school and the interests of the students. Additionally, the telephone conversation will generally give an initial reaction as to whether the person or company is appropriate. It is preferable if you know someone who is familiar with the person.

Upon finding a person or company that should be included in the file, enter the necessary information regarding them on the community resource card, and file it into the system. Ask the person to send any special pamphlets or brochures which the business or company may have available on the subject. If using the folder format, this information may be included in the folder. Additionally, consider including these brochures or pamphlets in the vertical file. If the library does not yet have a vertical file, this project offers an excellent opportunity to begin one.

One enthusiastic librarian used the Yellow Pages to put together the majority of the resources in her newly established file. She followed the following steps:

1. Make a list of the program topics to be included in the community resource file. For example: author, policeman.

2. Develop a format for the community resource card.

3. Jot down a list of questions to ask each person.

4. Set up a schedule for perusing the Yellow Pages. (For example, this librarian decided to cover two letters of the alphabet per week.)

5. Go through the listings for a particular letter and check the topics which would relate to school programming.

6. Set aside about 15-30 minutes a day during which to contact the sources by telephone. Hopefully, a volunteer who enjoys such a task can be found.

Remember to retain this particular edition of the Yellow Pages for future references. Make notations concerning the companies which do not have speakers or materials available to the schools. These Yellow Pages may need to be referred to in the future when updating and adding to the community resource file.

Media — Television, Radio, and Newspapers

Librarians should also be aware of program ideas and community resources generated through the media. Television, radio, newspapers, and magazines can inform librarians about people in the community who are available for speaking engagements.

Local television talk shows and educational television offer possible ideas for new resources to tap. Additionally, the Sunday newspaper often contains a listing of special events within the community such as films and plays, museum exhibits, art exhibits, musical events, holiday celebrations, and speakers which may correspond to special events at the school level.

While examining the cultural arts section of the Sunday newspaper, one librarian noted that a renowned children's author would be speaking at the local university. This librarian contacted the university and made arrangements for her student library volunteers to attend the session.

Public Libraries

Don't overlook the public libraries as a means for identifying resources. Many of the public libraries offer superb programs to the public throughout the year which are dependent upon community resources. At the same time, remember that the resources which the public library uses may also be available to the school. Make a note of any interesting programs presented by the public library as this information may be added to the library's community resource file. It is worth contacting these potential resources to determine whether they can be added to the community resource file in your school.

Since many public libraries take advantage of the local resources for their own programming, these libraries often establish their own community resource files. School librarians will find these community resource files extremely helpful. Examine this information and note interesting resource possibilities for your school's file. Of particular help, this file may offer unique categories of resources which might otherwise be overlooked. For example, a middle school librarian interested in a program for her students had not considered the local sports organizations in the area. Upon searching the local public library's file, she realized the benefits her students could gain from a program highlighting sports stars (see chapter 4). At the same time, she noted the various references to the area garden clubs and decided a program on gardening would also interest the middle school students. These topics, which otherwise might not have been thought of, could prove valuable for most school files.

Government Agencies

Government agencies at the city, state, and national levels can prove to be outstanding sources for library programs. While many of the government agencies can be located by using the local telephone directory, the *U.S. Government Manual* (GPO, annual) can help librarians locate other government resources. If fortunate enough to live near a U.S. government bookstore, go inside and discover all the interesting material available for programs and the library's vertical file. The bookstore may even have a manager who would be willing to present a program to students on information available from the U.S. government.

Aside from the print materials for the vertical file, the librarian will want to include a number of government agencies in the community resource file for possible program speakers and field trips. Tour the National Aeronautics and Space Administration (NASA) facility nearest your school, spend a day in court observing the district attorney's office at work, take a trip to the state capitol, tour the local police or fire department, or better yet, arrange for a speaker from one of the government agencies to present a program at the school.

When examining the government agencies for possible programming ideas, place NASA near the top of the list. Those librarians fortunate enough to live near a NASA facility will find a multitude of resources available. Besides welcoming students on field trips, NASA will provide speakers and exhibits for school programs.

Don't forget the military branches of government. Nearly every community has some type of military installation within easy reach, even if it is only a national guard unit. Each of the military branches can offer interesting presentations to the schools. One librarian used several U.S. Air Force and U.S. Navy pilots for a special eighth-grade program which highlighted military aviation. Each guest speaker brought exhibits to be shared with the students—a parachute, helmet, oxygen mask, maps, model planes, and uniforms. A slide show depicting the various types of military aircraft and an informal question-and-answer period marked the beginning of numerous follow-up events within each classroom. The school was filled with aviation enthusiasts for the next month, and no books related to aviation remained on the library shelves.

Other federal government agencies such as the Federal Bureau of Investigation (FBI), U.S. Department of Agriculture, and the U.S. Postal Service offer equally interesting possibilities. Occasionally, you can arrange for a postal worker or FBI agent to present a program for your student body. The Department of Agriculture at the federal and state levels offers valuable enrichment concerning soil conservation, ecology, and other related topics.

One innovative librarian at a newly opened elementary school invited a postal worker to her school for a special program entitled "The Post Office and You." The postal worker addressed such topics as: what happens to a letter after it is mailed; the importance of zip codes; and the necessity of addressing envelopes legibly. As an extra bonus the postal worker shared information about stamp collecting and informed the students about the special stamps put out monthly by the post office for collectors.

Until this program, the librarian had not considered the need for a vertical file in the library. After noting the enthusiasm for the program, the librarian felt this would be a good time to organize a school-wide campaign to set up a vertical file. Since many classroom teachers were already using this library program as a springboard to letter-writing activities, the librarian started a program involving the students in the creation of the vertical file. Each student in the fourth, fifth, and sixth grades was given an address to contact by letter requesting information which would eventually be included in the file. The librarian, teachers, and parent volunteers compiled a list of addresses which included state capitals, chambers of commerce in large cities, special tourist attractions, and a multitude of other resources. The real-life experience in writing letters meant more to the students than a classroom exercise. After receiving an answer to their requests at their home mailboxes, the students delivered the information to their teachers. In all, the experience was memorable and the benefits derived from the program far exceeded the original expectations. The children became informed about the jobs of the postal workers and the activities of the postal services, and they also learned the practical and necessary skill of letter writing. The letters they received ultimately resulted in the beginnings of a vertical file. The project presented teachers with a good, practical opportunity to teach letter writing. After playing a big part in obtaining the information for the vertical file, the students were eager to make use of it.

Consulates and embassies located in major cities often welcome inquiries from the public. Referenced in the telephone directory, a simple telephone call may open doors to fascinating social studies materials.

Using printed resource material obtained from the U.S. Department of Immigration, a middle school librarian in Louisiana developed a program highlighting guests who were refugees from Vietnam, Laos, and Cuba. Through slides, photographs, and informal discussions, each of the guests presented a view of the life and government within their homelands. After listening to these descriptions of the hardships faced by others in our world, the students gained a realization of how fortunate they were to live under a democratic government.

The U.S. Department of Naturalization can also present the students with information about how one becomes a citizen. Librarians may arrange for a person from this government agency to speak at the school, as well as a person taking part in the naturalization process. In fact, some of the students may be in the process of becoming citizens and would be excellent sources for input in such programs.

The Federal Aviation Administration (FAA), an often overlooked resource, can be used in conjunction with additional resources provided by local airlines. For a program which focused upon commercial aviation, one librarian invited three guest speakers to the library: an FAA controller, an airline pilot, and a private pilot. Using slides and other audiovisual aids, the guests described their unique skills. As a follow-up activity, some of the teachers arranged class tours to the nearby FAA facility. Other classrooms toured the airport and control tower.

At the state government level, wildlife and fish departments are usually eager to send speakers to the schools. Using audiovisual materials, such departments share knowledge of hunting and fishing regulations as well as wildlife preservation. Game wardens and wildlife and fish personnel often enjoy participating in career day programs.

Community resources on the local government level can be a starting point for enriching the government curriculum in our schools. Try to arrange a visit to the school by the mayor or council members. Students enjoy asking city officials questions about government. One high school librarian invited the mayor of her small town to the library one Friday morning. Students were encouraged to drop by the library during that period and visit informally with the mayor. To the librarian's surprise, many students who rarely visited the library arrived for the session.

Teachers frequently use the local police and fire departments in class-room programs. While field trips to the facilities are quite common, librarians can develop challenging programs around these public services. For example, one librarian invited a detective from the police station to demonstrate fingerprinting and discuss his job. Students eagerly questioned the guest, curious to learn more about the intriguing cases which the detective had solved. Another enterprising librarian scheduled local firemen to arrive at school during National Fire Prevention Week in a fire truck. After enjoying a tour of the truck, the first graders gathered in the library for a brief presentation by a firefighter, who was also a parent of one of the students.

Institutions

When developing a community resource file, librarians should examine the host of institutions within their community. For example, hospitals sometimes offer special programs to acquaint the students with topics such as nutrition, drugs, alcohol, depression, cleanliness, and health care. A simple telephone call to a major hospital can produce a multitude of program ideas not previously considered. Additionally, doctors and nurses are often willing to discuss their professions with students on career days.

Zoos, museums, planetariums, botanical gardens, and nature centers can also play an important role in program development. Not only are these institutions generally more than happy to send brochures to a school, they sometimes have people available to speak to student groups.

By examining special displays, exhibits, and activities at local universities or colleges, the librarian can often come up with a number of creative program possibilities. Special speakers participating in programs at the colleges may provide additional possibilities. A local university may be able to arrange for a professor in a specialized field to visit the school.

Search the cultural arts for possible resource materials, perhaps planning a program around a ballet troupe, opera star, or theater group. In many cases a small fee is involved for these programs, but it is usually well worth the cost.

Companies and Businesses

By calling upon local companies and businesses within the community, librarians can derive enrichment for our students. Many of the large companies have a public relations department which arranges speakers for schools. Through a single telephone call, the librarian can determine the type of programs and resources available. The program may include an audiovisual presentation, panel discussion, lecture, demonstration, workshop, or exhibit.

Some examples of companies and businesses which a librarian could look for in the Yellow Pages are:

telephone companies	shipping companies
electric companies	boat and yacht businesses
gas companies	major grocery stores
aircraft companies	ethnic food stores
computer companies	restaurants
major airlines	drug stores
travel agencies	railroad companies
bookstores	pet stores

In preparing a library program which focused upon cultures of the world, one librarian made use of numerous resources from his community resource file. First, he selected four cultures which were represented in the school population—Vietnamese, Mexican, Philippino, and Japanese. Then he examined the community resource file and made arrangements with parents from these cultures who had offered to share their experiences with the children. Next, the librarian once again consulted the community resource file to find the local businesses—airlines, travel agencies, embassies, local ethnic restaurants—related to these four cultures.

After scheduling the program for a two-day schedule, the librarian assigned a thirty-minute period for each class in the school to attend the event, which consisted of the four ethnic centers. As the students rotated from center to center, they listened to the guest speaker from the specific culture. While some centers included slide shows, others simply displayed photographs and maps of the country. Posters, pamphlets, and maps on the countries, donated by airlines and travel agencies, were also highlighted. As an added treat, several ethnic food stores provided a sampling of foods from each country. Additionally, representatives from the Mexican and Japanese consulates were on hand to give the students further information on the countries.

Organizations and Clubs

Various organizations and clubs within each community enjoy sharing a wide assortment of materials and activities with library programs. Identification and location of these organizations and clubs usually begins with word of mouth from friends, students, and teachers. Again, the Yellow Pages and the media may aid in locating these resources.

Although teachers and librarians realize young people have a special interest in sports, they rarely consider asking professional and amateur sports organizations to participate in school programs. The interest stirred by these organizations can be overwhelming. Librarians fortunate enough to live in an area with a major league baseball team should contact the organization to determine if players can speak at schools. Additionally, consider contacting local football, basketball, and hockey teams.

The smaller sports clubs—yachting, polo, soccer, volleyball, kayaking, canoeing, skiing, rodeo riding, and jogging—can also offer worthwhile program material. Many sports may not have a formal club, and contacts will have to be made by getting names of people on specific teams who would be interested in speaking to groups of students. Some librarians have turned to members of high school sports organizations for top-notch programs at the elementary and middle school levels. Don't overlook women's sport organizations when planning the programs.

Community organizations such as garden clubs can offer some unique program ideas. For example, one garden club sent three members out to a school for a "Botanical Delights" program (see chapter 4). Discussion of bromeliads, bonsai plants, and African violets generated student interest in plants.

While some librarians have turned to the chamber of commerce for program ideas, other community clubs and organizations can prove equally as valuable. Consider the following:

service clubs	computer clubs
historical society	gourmet clubs
orchid clubs	political organizations
nature clubs	bird watching clubs
ecology clubs	hobbies and special interest clubs
animal clubs	book clubs
symphony	art leagues

Don't forget the organizations which deal with a specific disease or medical problem. For example, the American Heart Association and the American Cancer Society can provide outstanding resources for the school programs spotlighting health.

Clubs or organizations pertaining to hobbies such as stamp collecting, shell collecting, comic book collecting, and gardening can provide interesting program material. Speakers from these groups often enjoy sharing their knowledge with students.

While historical societies and foundations generally can provide information about the community's past, they also may prove valuable for field trip resources. Symphony and art leagues can expose students to culture by providing exhibits, speakers and performers for the schools.

These interest groups can be extremely specialized and too numerous to mention. Pet clubs may focus upon anything from bulldogs to boas. Likewise, hobby groups may range in interest from coin collecting to baseball card collecting. Regardless of the group, its resources may prove valuable to the innovative librarian.

Special Events

Unique community events present librarians with resource material and ideas for program themes. For instance, during the Houston Livestock Show and Rodeo each year, many schools develop their own programs around the rodeo theme. Why not consider extending the celebration of other community events such as athletic events, holidays, and festivals into the school library? Such events have already been promoted by the media, and the librarian will find it quite easy to promote interest within the school. By helping the community support rodeos, fishing tournaments, an olympic festival, Cinco de Mayo Day, and other festive events, librarians can make the library an exciting place. Call upon the community for print and nonprint materials as well as speakers to help incorporate the event into the curriculum. By working together with community leaders, the librarian will play a part in creating a strong bond between the school and the community.

Displays and Exhibits

When planning library programs, be creative and find alternatives to speakers. Programs which highlight special displays or exhibits can entice students to the library. Identify these displays and exhibits when you initially contact the people and organizations within your community. Inquire as to whether they have exhibits or displays related to the topic. Likewise, when sending questionnaires to the parents, ask if they have any items or collections to share for displays or exhibits.

Some companies and organizations make special audiovisual productions available to the schools. For example, several wildlife organizations share their knowledge of wildlife preservation through free films.

Mini-museum features the Chinese New Year. The P.T.A. provided materials for this exhibit to correspond with the local celebration of the holiday. Reproduced with permission of the Clear Creek Independent School District, League City, Texas.

ARRANGING THE COMMUNITY
RESOURCE FILE

After deciding upon the format for the community resource file, locating resources, and recording the information on the cards, the next step is deciding on the arrangement of the cards within the filing system.

Arrangement of the resource cards alphabetically by subject or topic usually proves to be the most advantageous. Since the majority of library programs will probably focus upon a special theme, an arrangement by subject will prove beneficial. Additionally, cross-referencing names of speakers and organizations to the subjects proves helpful. By making a listing of subject headings, it will be much easier to use the file.

UPDATING THE COMMUNITY RESOURCE FILE

As librarians make use of the community resources, it is important they record the date and some information about the presentation for future reference. Some librarians record this information on the back of the card. If anything critical is to be said about a particular resource, it should be recorded in a confidential file or some sort of coded system should be used. This information will prove helpful for future programs, as a librarian would not want to invite back to the school a speaker who couldn't relate to the students. Perhaps a resource was not appropriate for a particular age group, or could not communicate well with the audience. It is important to check on this information before scheduling a guest; however, this sometimes proves impossible.

At the beginning of each school year, update the entire resource file. After sending a questionnaire to the students' parents, be certain to take the time to update this information. Review all entries, regardless of whether or not they have been utilized. Contact the persons or organizations already within the resource file. Weed out those entries which are no longer valid. Keep up with the file, or it may become too difficult to manage.

FINDING TIME FOR A COMMUNITY RESOURCE FILE

A major concern for librarians is how to find time for the telephoning and organizing involved in a community resource file. A good way is to utilize the volunteer workers in the library, most of whom are parents. The remainder of this chapter deals with establishing a good parent volunteer program. Without volunteers or aides, a librarian will rarely be able to find time to plan library programs, much less establish a community resource file.

RECRUITING VOLUNTEERS TO
HELP WITH PROGRAMMING

Without those parents who give freely of their time, many school activities simply could not occur. The library is certainly one important place within the school which needs volunteers, particularly if the school does not have a library aide. With proper training, parent volunteers can help keep the library running smoothly on a daily basis.

By taking over certain routine duties, parent volunteers allow the librarian time to plan special library programs for the students. Also, these volunteers can participate in many aspects of program development and

Volunteers performing routine tasks free the librarian for more creative activities. Reproduced with permission of the Clear Creek Independent School District, League City, Texas.

production. Parent volunteers can lend a helping hand by developing learning centers for the students, hanging student art exhibits, and setting up special exhibits. During programs, volunteers can help with traffic flow.

One Texas librarian attributed much of the success of her program, "Carnival of Fun," to the parent volunteers. After arranging for a magician, a puppeteer, and a juggler to perform for the primary students, the librarian called upon parents to help with traffic flow. Costumed as clowns, volunteers ushered the students to each of the three carnival stages and made certain that they rotated to the next stage at the proper time. Later in the school year when the P.T.A. sponsored a "Circus Exhibit" to correlate with the arrival of the Ringling Brothers' Circus, the volunteers again made use of the costumes. This time the volunteers acted as ushers to keep traffic moving smoothly past the exhibits. At the same time, these clowns monitored the items on exhibit, providing unobtrusively the necessary element of security.

Many of the parent volunteers enjoy sharing their skills and talents with the students. For instance, one mother who seemed to always find time each week to work in the library received high praises for her cake decorating abilities. During a special library program, "Cooking with a Flair," this talented parent awed students with a demonstration of the art of cake decorating.

Parent volunteers can also play an important role in helping librarians develop a community resource file. After devising a set of questions for potential community resources, the librarian may decide to leave the telephoning to parent volunteers. The volunteer can also be responsible for recording the information on the community resource card.

How does a librarian find the parents? There are several things to keep in mind when starting a parent volunteer program. First, the principal's permission for the volunteer program must be obtained. While some principals will be hesitant about volunteers roaming about their schools, the majority will welcome the added help. If the former is the case, employ the approach of persistent diplomacy. Meet with the principal, prepared to illustrate specific tasks which volunteers will assist in accomplishing. Try to cite examples of other libraries where the volunteer program resulted in positive gains for the school. Be willing to compromise. Start small and, if necessary, request permission to use only one or two volunteers. Remember the best defense is a well-prepared offense.

After obtaining the principal's permission, try to establish the parent volunteer program through the P.T.A. If the organization can appoint a chairman for the library, it will be much easier to start a reliable volunteer program. Hopefully, the librarian will participate in the selection of the chairman, as working with a chairman who agrees with your philosophies increases the chances of a successful volunteer program. This chairman knows the parents and will play a key role in recruiting volunteers who are reliable. While it is best if most of this recruiting is done through the P.T.A., circumstances may require that librarians do their own recruiting. In this case, it may be desirable to send notices, such as that in figure 11, to the parents in the school to determine who is available.

A goal of twenty volunteers will provide adequate assistance in maintaining the library. If possible, assign two volunteers to each half day period of the week. Some librarians may find that twenty volunteers is an unrealistic goal for their particular situation and will have to settle for what they can get. Regardless of whether the library has five or thirty volunteers, throw a celebration for volunteers during the first few weeks of school — it could be a coffee, a tea, or a luncheon. Meet the volunteers and let them know what a special role they play in the school. At this party, give them a questionnaire to complete concerning their interests (see figure 12, page 64). With this input, the task of assigning jobs to volunteers will be much easier. In order to keep volunteers, never assign them a job they dislike — even if it means a job for yourself. All too often, volunteers tend to get the dull, unenjoyable tasks. The party for volunteers presents an excellent opportunity to escort the volunteers on a tour of the library facility. At this point, they'll begin to get acquainted with basic library procedures.

Above all, make dependability a necessary requirement for the job. At the first meeting, stress the necessity of letting the librarian or P.T.A. know as far in advance as possible if they cannot serve on their assigned day. A benefit of assigning two volunteers to each half day period is the probability that at least one person will be present to cover the duties.

Some school libraries enjoy the benefits of a substitute volunteer program. When regular volunteers find it impossible to make their assigned duty days, they call upon a substitute. Since substitute volunteers play an important part in the library program, include them on the guest list for all volunteer celebrations, orientation tours, and training workshops.

Dear Parents:

Our school library needs your help. To keep the library functioning at its maximum potential, our library depends heavily upon parent volunteers. These volunteers make it possible to carry out unique library activities and programs. Would you be willing to work in the library several hours a week: If not, do you have some special skills you could perform at home? Please complete the following questionnaire if you are interested in volunteering.

- -

LIBRARY VOLUNTEER FORM

Name: _____   Days & Times Available to
                               Work in Library:
Address: _____

_____   _____

Phone: _____   _____

Name(s) of Child(ren):   Teacher:

_____   _____

_____   _____

Special Skills/Talents/Interests:

_____ Typing   _____ Processing books/
                                      magazines
_____ Artwork/Graphics
                              _____ Book repair
_____ Laminating
                              _____ Set up exhibits
_____ Filing
                              _____ Other (describe)
_____ Read Aloud
                                      _____
_____ Storytelling
                                      _____

_____ I cannot work in the library, but I am willing to do work at
        home.
        Type of work: _____

Fig. 11. School library needs volunteers.

VOLUNTEER TASK REQUEST

Volunteer's Name: _____

Phone: _____

Days & Times Available: _____

Please check the library tasks which most interest you:

_____ Typing (letters, catalog cards, books cards, etc.)

_____ Work at circulation desk

_____ Laminating

_____ Help to process books

_____ Help to process magazines

_____ Help develop learning centers

_____ Community resource file (contact resources & record information)

_____ Repair damaged books

_____ Shelve books

_____ Read shelves

_____ Read stories aloud

_____ Storytelling

_____ Process audiovisual materials

_____ Maintain vertical file

_____ Supervise reference area

_____ Assist with displays & exhibits

_____ File cards

Fig. 12. Volunteer task request (to be given to volunteers after their orientation tour).

CONCLUSION

People, places, things all can work as key elements in the process of library programming. Do not feel overwhelmed. Consider this chapter as a menu from which to select. Use those ideas which appeal to you, reserve others for future use. Just as a librarian cannot buy every book, neither can every resource be tapped. And although some resources will not want to participate, there are still many from which to choose. A wealth of resources can be found in the community which will greatly expand the library's role in the educational process through programming.

4

Something for Everyone
Model Library Programs That Work

ELEMENTARY LEVEL PROGRAMS

"Fascinating Futures"

"What are you going to be when you grow up?" Judith Plummer, an elementary school librarian, decided to help her students search for answers through a program called "Fascinating Futures." The community resource file proved useful in helping the librarian find interesting people willing to share information about their jobs. After considering student interests as well as the available choices, the librarian chose to highlight four occupations—an artist, a military and commercial airline pilot, a chef, and a police detective. Although the use of speakers from the community is common in many schools, the uniqueness of this library program lay in the manner in which the librarian presented the program.

After following the steps suggested in chapter 2, Judith submitted her program plans to the school principal for approval. Impressed with the positive public relations the program could bring to the school, the principal readily agreed to the program plans which included:

1. Objectives
    a. To promote the library.
    b. To introduce the students to four "fascinating" occupations.

2. Procedures/Methods
    a. Four speakers will discuss and demonstrate their jobs.
    b. Speakers will give students a short question-and-answer period.
    c. Books related to special careers will be displayed.

After several weeks of publicizing the upcoming event, Judith invited the entire elementary school to the program. Since the program was aimed at the entire student body, scheduling proved the most critical factor in programming. In order for the children to experience the program in small groups, the librarian scheduled it on two consecutive mornings. (Librarians may find it difficult to schedule the same guests on two consecutive days and instead may have to schedule different people for different days.) This librarian used an interest center approach, establishing a center for each of the four occupations, one in each corner of the media center. The four programs took place simultaneously, with each group of students spending fifteen minutes at a center before rotating to the next center. Parent volunteers supervised the rotation from center to center and also reminded classes when to come to the media center.

Each center, colorfully decorated according to the appropriate topic, enticed the children to share in unique experiences. The artist center, which spotlighted a local artist who demonstrated silk screening, was decorated with silk screens as well as arts and crafts books from the library. Although only a few students actually participated in the demonstration due to time constraints, the artist made certain each child received a sample of silk screen art.

Students entering the flying center encountered a suspended parachute, model airplanes hanging from the ceiling, flight maps, and aviation books. Here, the children met an Air National Guard and commercial airline pilot who allowed ample time for questions. They left the center with souvenir pilot wings and model airplanes.

The backdrop of the cooking center included displays of antique cooking utensils and cookbooks from the library. In this center, the children met a chef from a local restaurant who demonstrated making pretzels. The students were given an opportunity to knead the dough and shape a pretzel. Chef Simone gave each child a recipe and a pretzel.

In the detective center, children heard stories of the daily adventures of a detective. The various objects on display included a fingerprinting kit and detective informational books from the library. The detective talked informally to the students and answered many questions. Having only enough time to fingerprint a few of the students, the detective left the fingerprint kit in the detective center and invited the students back during their free time to make their own fingerprints.

Judging from the positive response to the formal evaluation forms given teachers, this program definitely succeeded in accomplishing its goals. Both teachers and students asked for more programs of this nature. Likewise, parents and administrators expressed their enthusiasm. Most importantly, the program promoted library usage and established good public relations between the school and community. The children gained knowledge of the world around them and became aware of the school library as a center for special materials and people as well as books.

"Crafts Jamboree"

A sign stating: Help! Student Suggestions Requested! appeared above the library suggestion box during the first week of the school year. All students were encouraged to complete a suggestion form (see figure 1, page 11) concerning books or library programs they would enjoy. By asking for input, David Dugas hoped to make the students feel more a part of his total library program.

Noting the large number of students who requested programs on arts and crafts, David began planning a "Crafts Jamboree" in the media center during School Library Week. By highlighting special craftspersons at work he hoped to encourage children to use the library. His plans included:

1. Objectives

    a. To interest "nonlibrary users" in reading books for leisure.

    b. To acquaint students with various crafts which could be enjoyed at leisure.

2. Procedures/Methods

    a. Talks by various craftspersons.

    b. Demonstrations by craftspersons.

    c. Book displays.

With the help of the questionnaire (see figure 9, page 46) and the community resource file, David located parents of students within the school who had special talents which they were willing to share. Upon contacting the parents, he made the following suggestions:

- If possible, bring items, including some at various stages of completion, to share.

- Supply posters and diagrams depicting the history of and giving background information on the craft.

- If the program lends itself to it, allow time for student participation.

- If appropriate, have something for the students to keep as a souvenir of their visit. The souvenir may be as simple as instructions for the art or craft activity or the product itself.

David also made it clear to the parent volunteers that he would help set up displays and provide handouts for the children, if the speaker could supply a master copy in advance.

Publicity for the Crafts Jamboree began several weeks prior to the event. Students helped make posters and flyers which were passed out in the classrooms. Excitement began to build.

Each day of the program week focused upon three crafts, and classes were encouraged to sign up daily to visit the craft centers which appealed to them. Each of these centers, located in three corners of the media center, featured a craftsperson who demonstrated a craft and presented a 10-minute talk about it. Some guests displayed items at various stages of completion, while others displayed a variety of completed items. Student participation was encouraged in each center. For example, the pottery worker gave all visitors to the pottery center clay to shape. Many of the guests used audio-visual aids (pictures, charts, slides) to further the learning experience. At some of the craft centers, children received souvenirs such as quilting instructions or a sample piece of pottery.

The schedule for the week of library events included a wide array of "happenings" (see figure 13).

During the week following the program, David was pleased to find the teachers were extending the program into their classrooms. While many focused upon the crafts for classroom projects, others encouraged their students to research the arts and crafts. A few classes had their own Crafts Jamboree which highlighted student art and craft projects. Each class selected a guest, and wrote notes of appreciation.

	Monday	Tuesday	Wednesday	Thursday	Friday
Center 1	Quilting	Spinning	Glass blowing	Easter egg painting	Sail making
Center 2	Pottery	Wood-working	Macrame	Weaving	Silk screening
Center 3	Sculpture	Hat making	Wood-carving	Model ship building	Model airplane building

Fig. 13. Week of library events.

While the entire student body reaped benefits from the program, the greatest reward for David came from encouraging students to check books out of the library for pleasure. Through programs such as these, students at the elementary level come to look upon reading as fun and therefore take a step toward becoming lifetime readers.

Various alternatives exist for the format of this program. The selection of crafts will depend upon the resources available in the community and the librarian's needs and interests. Due to class scheduling the librarian may find it necessary to invite the craftsperson for only two to three hours rather than a full day, while other participants will be willing to be present more than one day. Fewer or additional centers may be more beneficial for some libraries.

Occasionally scheduling for a full week period makes this event impossible. In this case, a large number of the guests could come on one special day to participate in the Crafts Jamboree. This program could take place in various areas of the school. The participants, stationed in various locations of the school, could share their talents with the children throughout the day. Classes could rotate from one area to another and participate in numerous activities of their choice. In this case, the librarian would distribute a map of the center locations to each classroom to make the program run more smoothly. A major drawback of a one-day jamboree, however, is the difficulty of involving all of the students.

For David's program, the teachers were invited to take their entire class to the jamboree at the scheduled time. A variation on this type of program would provide for voluntary participation on the part of each student. Such programs can serve as incentives for students to complete their work.

"Gifted Storytellers"

Storytime usually brings to mind read-aloud sessions. In *Read Aloud Handbook* (Penguin, 1985), Jim Trelease describes the educational gains made by children whose teachers and parents read to them. This valuable guide also offers librarians and classroom teachers a bibliography of books certain to keep the interest of students. However, with so much emphasis upon read-aloud programs, another important alternative to storytime — storytelling — is often ignored. Librarians should search the community for gifted storytellers, as they have a special gift which should be shared with children.

Good storytellers are not easy to find. Sending out a questionnaire to students' parents at the beginning of each school year (see figure 9, page 46) can help locate storytellers, for there are often parents or grandparents in the school community who are eager to share their talents. On the other hand, storytellers in the community may be located through the community resource file in the public library or from information received at meetings of professional organizations. Consider using the professional storytellers within the local area. Their fee is usually quite justifiable when weighed against the benefits received from the storytelling session.

Donna Fay, an elementary librarian in Arizona, found that many of the teachers, particularly teachers in grades four through six, did not have a regularly scheduled storytime. Realizing the educational values of story-times, the librarian initiated a year-long "Gifted Storytellers" program in the media center. Donna had only one main objective: to interest children in literature. By taking advantage of the information gained from her community resource file, she located storytellers for an on-going library program. These gifted storytellers included parents, grandparents, and community residents.

The librarian began the program by announcing that on each Friday afternoon from 1:00 to 1:30 the library would feature a storyteller, who would share a story with the students. Primary grades and upper grades would alternate weeks for this program. While teachers were invited to bring their entire classes to the sessions, individual students with permission from their teachers were also welcome. However, to avoid having too many students at one session, teachers choosing to bring entire classes to the program were asked to select a session and to note it on the "Storyteller's Calendar." If the calendar indicated that requests outnumbered the space available, Donna would find it necessary to schedule several storytelling sessions. Library classes and other activities such as research continued to take place in the library during this time.

Using her creative talents, Donna arranged a corner of the library for the storytelling period. A comfortable rocking chair, brightly colored rug, and pillows were placed in the corner. Anticipating that some storytellers would prefer to sit on the floor or to stand, the arrangement of the corner was left flexible. In addition, she also found the corner was a perfect area for her puppet stage and puppets.

Donna realized the importance of advertising her library programs. At faculty meetings, she reminded teachers of the storytelling period. An easel at the library entrance announced the name of the next storyteller, the title of the story, the date, and the time. Various types of stories were scheduled, including tales from other lands, fairy tales, scary stories, mysteries, funny stories, and holiday stories.

From the beginning, teachers and students showed enthusiastic support for the event. Donna also found that by alternating weeks with primary and upper grades, the number of students at the sessions usually worked out fine. For most sessions, all classrooms did not choose to participate, thus keeping the sessions fairly small. For the few times during the year when all classrooms did sign up for one session, Miss Fay made arrangements in advance for the storyteller to stay for a second session from 1:30 to 2:00.

When Gifted Storytellers featured the school principal as the storyteller, all classes signed up to take part in the session and Miss Fay had to ask the principal if he would stay for a second session. The principal, impressed by the entire event, was more than happy to share his story during a second period.

Another memorable Gifted Storytellers event at Donna's school was a refugee's telling of the Vietnamese version of "Cinderella." Following the story, the children viewed a display of various objects from Vietnam.

After listening to several storytellers, students became aware of the tremendous amount of preparation involved in a storytelling session. Teachers encouraged students to share their own stories and some used the library corner for their own storytelling events. Children often used the puppets in their storytelling. Many prepared for telling a story by reading a book from the library, learning the story, and eventually sharing it with their class. The librarian soon found that some of the older students were telling stories to the younger children. Storytelling had become contagious in the school.

Because this library program proved so successful the first year, the librarian decided to expand it the following year. With the funding aid of the P.T.A., Donna scheduled a professional storyteller to present a full-day program at the school. Scheduling each classroom in the school for a special period was the most difficult part of this program (see chapter 2 for solutions to this problem). In Miss Fay's case, she allotted a forty-five-minute period to each grade, during which a professional storyteller shared a story as well as discussed the art of storytelling and answered questions.

Through this program, the elementary students came to view the library as the hub of the school—a place overflowing with interesting people, activities, and information.

If there is a college or university in your community, see if courses in storytelling are offered. Often professors who teach storytelling courses are anxious to locate field sites to provide practice for their students. If such arrangements can be made, the need for extra funds may be eliminated and the library may be inundated with excited storytellers.

MIDDLE SCHOOL LEVEL PROGRAMS

"International Festival"

The library shelves are overflowing with resources related to the cultures of the world. Unfortunately, many of these books are used only when social studies teachers require children to research a particular country or culture. Librarians at the elementary level often use world cultures as a theme for library programs. However, due to the structure of class schedules at middle school level, these school librarians tend to discount library programming. Nonetheless, students in grades six through eight are quite curious about life in other countries and librarians can further interest them in reading about other cultures by using activities which originate in the library.

An "International Festival" library program began with the librarian posting trivia questions throughout the school to arouse student interest. Tony Lowry, a librarian at a middle school, discovered that the more bizarre the question, the higher the interest level:

- In what country do the people drink the blood of cattle?

- What culture requires that a man must kill a lion before getting married?

- In what country do parents chop off the arms or hands of their children to make them good beggars?

These questions, along with a display of books which contained the answers, were the starting point of a big event. After finding that the students were coming to the library more and more to search for answers to the trivia questions, Tony carried the activities one step further the next year by designating one special week of the school year as "International Festival Week." During this week the library would highlight various cultures of the world. The plans for such a week included:

1. Objectives

   a. To make students aware of the multitude of materials available in the library on world cultures.

   b. To expand the students' knowledge of world cultures.

2. Procedures/Methods

   a. Display books on cultures.

   b. Presentations and demonstrations by guests representing eight cultures.

During the planning phase, Tony first shared his program plans with the principal and teachers at a faculty meeting. After obtaining their support he contacted the local travel agencies and airlines to get information, travel brochures, and posters. Using the community resource file, he discovered students' parents from other countries who were willing to share their cultures with the children. After deciding upon the particular cultures which would most interest the students, the librarian contacted eight of the parents listed in the community resource file. They agreed to participate, and a date was set for the five-day event. Next, Tony met with the eight parents and began planning the program. The parents suggested that they wear the costume of their country for the International Festival. They also agreed to bring items which represented their particular culture and to set up their own centers.

After fully publicizing the event, the International Festival got underway. The guests were scheduled to speak at various times throughout the week in the library. Students were given the schedule of events and invited to select the presentations which interested them. A sign-up sheet indicated how much space was available for participants. The guest speakers, all dressed in native costumes, presented a twenty-minute talk and allowed ten minutes for questions. They used a variety of approaches to interest the students in their cultures. For example, the Indian speaker entertained the group with sitar music, and served chapatty, an Indian bread. Other guests used maps of their countries as backdrops and displayed artifacts associated with the culture. A few of the speakers gave slide presentations of their homeland. All of these activities added to the atmosphere of the event and lured the students into the library.

Throughout the week, flyers and posters urged students to wear costumes from various countries on Friday, the last day of the "happening."

On Friday morning over half of the student body arrived in costumes. The culminating event of the week was a performance in the gymnasium by a local Greek folk dance group.

Throughout the week books were on exhibit to represent each of the eight countries highlighted. The cultural displays established by the guest speakers remained in the library for several weeks following the event. Tony encouraged students to browse the exhibits at their leisure.

The library program encouraged teachers to relate classroom activities to the "happening" in the library. During the week following the program, the seventh grade social studies teacher organized a treasure hunt. Students were given twenty-five questions regarding various cultures.

Although the success of the program was obvious, Tony asked the teachers to complete a formal evaluation of the program (see figure 14). The teachers asked for more programs of this nature, and offered some helpful criticism concerning future scheduling of library events.

The positive effects of the program continued for weeks following the event. Students continued to enjoy the exhibits in the library and eagerly checked out material on the world cultures. The highest praise for the program was by students, continually asking: "When are we going to do it again? It was so much fun."

"Botanical Delights Festival"

After completing a weekly or monthly circulation count, do certain categories of books appear to have a low circulation rate? How can librarians encourage students to check out these books? After noting the low circulation statistics in the plant and gardening books, a librarian at Jenkins Middle School in Washington decided to see if a library program could influence the check-out rate of these books.

Using the theme "Botanical Delights," Julie Katz and her parent volunteers began planning a two-day program about three months in advance. Her major plans included:

1. Objectives

   a. To interest students in reading informational books about gardening and plants.

   b. To provide students with a knowledge of gardening and plants.

   c. To increase the library circulation rate.

LRC PROGRAM EVALUATION

Please take a few moments to help me access the recent LRC program.

1 = disagree   2 = no opinion   3 = agree

1. The program was well organized   _____

2. The program related to our educational   _____
   goals

3. The speaker was easy to understand and   _____
   held the students' attention

4. It was worthwhile for my students to   _____
   participate

5. Please continue to have special LRC   _____
   programs

I encourage you to tell me your thoughts and reactions beyond the above questions. Please use the space below. No signatures are necessary and please be very candid. Just return the form to my box in the office.

Reactions from your students:

Suggestions for improvement:

Sugestions for future program topics, resources, etc.:

Other:

Fig. 14. Sample program evaluation form for teachers.

2. Procedures/Methods

   a. Sponsor contests.

   b. Guest speakers will discuss their specific knowledge of gardening and plants.

   c. The guests will present demonstrations in their specialized areas of gardening.

In contacting the local arboretum and nature center to determine the resources available within the community, Julie found them eager to supply the school with pamphlets, posters, and packets filled with information regarding plant life. Additionally, they offered to help her make arrangements for a keynote speaker, who specialized in native plants, to take part in the program.

Needing more speakers for the event, Julie turned to the community resource file for help. After still failing to find enough resources on the topic, she investigated the resource file at the public library and located four speakers to share their knowledge of plants in four unique areas: making a bonsai tree, poisonous plants, herbs and spices, and flower arranging.

Publicity for the event began two months prior to the program. The students were informed the library was sponsoring contests during the "Botanical Delights Festival." The first contest, the "Most Beautiful Botanical Delight Contest," encouraged students to select a bulb plant they would like to enter in the contest. The rules stipulated the student plant the bulb in a container so it could later be taken to school, and to nurture and care for that plant for the two-month period prior to the contest. The contest rules also encouraged the students to learn as much as possible about the plant and to be prepared to talk about their "botanical delight" when interviewed. Other contests were also advertised.

Various books, posters, seed catalogs, and pamphlets were displayed in the library throughout the two-month period. More books on the subject were checked out during this time.

The program began with the keynote speaker, sponsored by the local nature center, who discussed the native plants of the local area. The students bombarded the speaker with questions. Other signs indicated a successful program. Over sixty entries in the "Most Beautiful Botanical Delight Contest" were displayed in the library, along with an index card giving the type of plant, the name of the student who cared for it, and a nickname for the plant. Nicknames for the bulbs included Oscar, Priscilla, Macbeth, and Herman. The winner of this contest was not revealed until the last day of the week.

Julie Katz sponsored two other contests to help gain interest in the "happening." One contest involved naming the librarian's favorite African violet, which was on display in the library during the week of the program. Another African violet was the prize for the student whose name — Drusilla — was drawn.

In another contest, pupils interested in photography were asked to enter photographs of plants in bloom. Around forty students entered the contest, and their pictures were exhibited in the library. A team of judges selected the best photograph, and awarded a bonsai tree to the winner.

Other highlights of the program week included botanical presentations which had been arranged on different days. Student and teacher attendance was strictly voluntary. The schedule for programs included:

- Monday: "Our Native Plants" (keynote address).

- Tuesday: "Poisonous Plants — BEWARE!"

- Wednesday: "Herbs and Spices — Delightful Treats."

- Thursday: "Flower Arrangements — Gifts to the Eye."

- Friday: "The Making of a Bonsai Tree."

The most popular event of the week was the "Herbs and Spices" presentation by two amateur gardeners, who were located through the community resource file at the local library. These guests encouraged the students to smell and touch various herbs and spices during the sessions. After the presentation, students enjoyed the mint ice tea provided by the P.T.A.

Throughout the week, the middle school children visited the library to enjoy the plant displays arranged by their classmates. On the last day, two local "garden" radio hosts acted as judges for the "Most Beautiful Botanical Delight Contest" and after much discussion presented Ronald Counts with the grand prize for his magnificent iris.

Did Julie accomplish her original goal of increasing circulation rate in the plant category? Through book displays, contests, and guest speakers, the circulation rate increased by 40 percent during the months prior to and preceding the program and students continued to check out books in this category several months later. Formal evaluation forms completed by the teachers indicated that the program had enriched the curriculum. Many students began to consider gardening as a hobby and asked for particular books on the subject or requested that more books be ordered. One student became fascinated with orchids and read everything available on the subject. Some of the classrooms caught the fever and started their own vegetable gardens in patio pots. One project proved so successful that the class had a vegetable party to enjoy the fruits and vegetables of their labor. Some classrooms went on field trips to the local nature center to learn more.

After this successful event, Julie began making program plans for the next year, guaranteeing teachers and students they would like the next program even more.

"Meet the Sports Stars"

Unfortunately many leisure readers are lost during the middle school years. Heavy assignment loads, class scheduling, and social interests partially account for this lack of interest in reading. Additionally, due to curriculum requirements, librarians and teachers at this level put much of their time into meeting curriculum needs. There seems to be less time to emphasize reading for pleasure. Many students use the library only to complete reference work or to check out a required book. If a librarian's goal is indeed to develop lifetime readers, students need to be encouraged to read for sheer enjoyment. One means of accomplishing this goal lies in library programming.

Aware that many students who do not normally enjoy reading are interested in sports, librarian Pat Jackson met the challenge by planning a library program called "Meet the Sports Stars." Fortunate to live near a major city with several professional teams, she began calling the professional sports organizations as well as the amateur clubs to determine the resources that were available. Pat found that although some organizations would send sports stars out to the schools, the athletes were all booked up for the year. A parent of one of the students came to the rescue. This parent, a former major league baseball pitcher, was more than happy to give the school several hours of his time.

After scheduling this special guest, Pat began investigating the possibility of having more than one guest. Some of the local amateur organizations proved quite helpful. After numerous phone calls, Pat drafted eight representatives of local organizations for the program: a bicycling club, a polo team, a gymnastics group, a jogging club, a weight lifting club, a bowling league, a yachting club, and a local rodeo club. Both sexes were represented.

On the day prior to the program, Pat began arranging the facility. Teachers, students, and parents provided items for display such as photographs, sports equipment, and posters, which would remain in the library for several weeks following the program for the students to enjoy. The program also offered Pat an opportunity to showcase the library's sports books.

Over a two-day period the library program offered information and entertainment to the students interested in attending the sessions. For the opening event, Pat invited the entire school to attend a presentation by the former baseball pitcher. Other smaller sessions were scheduled throughout the day, for which individual students and classes had been requested to sign up in advance. On opening day four guests—a marathon runner, a state bowling champ, a former America's Cup team winner, and a competitive cyclist—were stationed in four areas of the library. They described their particular sport, how they became interested in that sport, how much time they devoted to it, and answered questions. Students and teachers rotated from one sports star to another.

On the second day of the festivities, classes were given their choice of sessions to attend. A gymnast and a weight lifter gave demonstrations while video tape and slide shows were shown on the rodeo and polo.

The two-day program culminated with these questions from the students: "Are we going to do it again next year?" "What sports stars will come next year?" "Do you have any books on polo?" and "Do you have any information on how I can join the bicycling club?" Few books about the sports related to this program remained on the shelves, and many students requested Pat to order more books on these topics.

Looking back over the major goals and methods of the program Pat was able to evaluate the program's success:

1. Objectives

    a. To encourage reading for sheer entertainment and pleasure.

    b. To make the students aware of the various sports books and audiovisual materials available for check out through the library.

    c. To inform students of the various sports activities in the community.

2. Procedures/Methods

    a. Discussion of particular sports by sports stars from the local community.

    b. Demonstration of various sports by local sports stars.

    c. Displays of sports-related books.

Pat's methods had proved successful. Judging from the students' enthusiasm and positive attitude toward the library, she had met her objectives. Furthermore, for weeks after the program Pat observed check outs by students who had seldom entered the library prior to the program. These students had discovered that reading can be fun if the subject is right.

HIGH SCHOOL LEVEL PROGRAMS

"Paperback Book Swap"

High school librarian Gayla Norris sensed that the students at her school did not perceive reading as a recreational activity. A sampling of the circulation records of fictional works in the library's collection reinforced her feelings. It seemed to her, also, that the demographics of the Jackson High School district might be contributing to the situation. Family income generally fell below the state median, and, to compound the problem, the local economy had slowed to such an extent that the unemployment rate was in double digit figures. The library budget seemed to shrink each year, thus limiting the purchase of books which might satisfy the students' pleasure reading needs. In an effort to spotlight and promote leisure reading, Gayla outlined an idea for a "Paperback Book Swap." The program would center around paperback books that the students had read and would like to exchange for some other title. She prepared a general outline of the program to present to the principal and English faculty for approval and suggestions. The basic components included the following:

1. Objectives

    a. To encourage reading for pleasure.

    b. To make new titles available to students at no cost.

    c. To generate (if some books were not claimed) some extra funds for purchase of library materials.

2. Procedures/Methods

    a. Distribution through the English classes of the announcement and information about participation in the program (including an explanation for parents).

    b. Collection of books in the library and issuing of book claim tickets for use in claiming new books (students receiving one ticket for two books).

    c. Evaluation of all books contributed to eliminate any inappropriate material prior to distribution.

    d. Redistribution of books through the use of the tickets issued to students and students selecting from the books collected.

Discussions with both the principal and the English faculty elicited enthusiastic support. Some pertinent questions arose such as: "What will evaluation mean?" and "Why will the students receive only one ticket for two books?" Gayla explained that the flyers announcing the program would include the explanation that all books brought in would be accepted but there might be some books whose condition would be such that they would not be suitable for inclusion in the swap. Further, some students might contribute titles that would fall outside the school's approved selection policy and she did not wish to include these titles in the swap. However, tickets would be issued to the students bringing such material so as not to penalize them.

Receiving approval to proceed with the program, Gayla prepared the flyer in figure 15 for distribution to the students.

While preparing the flyer, Gayla also prepared the swap tickets, using leftover orange paper to make the tickets more distinctive. She formatted a master consisting of twelve tickets, then loaded the colored paper into the copier. She enlisted the help of a library aide to cut and box the tickets until

---

FREE READS—"NEW" BOOKS FOR OLD!

Do you have paperback books at home that you have read and would like to trade for some other paperback? If so, then bring them to the library during the weeks of February 3-7 and February 10-14. We will issue you one swap-ticket for every two · books you contribute. Then beginning February 21 you may come in and make your selection (one book per ticket) from the "Book Swap Shelves." **Do not lose your ticket(s). You must have it to claim your selection(s).** The books that are not selected will be sold for 10 cents. All funds from this sale will help buy new books for your library.

Please share this information with your parents.

Fig. 15. Free reads.

time to begin distribution. A teacher in the graphics department graciously agreed to arrange for the preparation of five large colored posters advertising the program. Gayla hung the signs in various high traffic areas of the school, saving one to post at the entrance of the library. She located two large, sturdy boxes to place behind the circulation desk. As students brought in their books to exchange for tickets, the paperbacks could be quickly dropped in these boxes.

During the two-week collection period, the boxes behind the circulation desk began to fill and Gayla began the sorting process. Books which were in poor condition (covers missing, sections of pages missing, etc.) were discarded immediately. Also discarded were a few volumes which were pornographic (as defined by the Library Selection Policy). However, the students who had brought these paperbacks were neither identified nor penalized, having received their tickets solely on the basis on the number of paperbacks they brought to the desk. At the end of the two-week collection period, Gayla found she had accumulated 786 usable paperback books and had distributed 412 tickets. She had sorted most of the books as they arrived and the interim week provided sufficient time to complete the sorting process.

On the first day of the swap, she placed 200 of the books on the swap shelves—a library cart arrangement near the circulation desk—trying to provide a variety of types of books in the group. The person collecting the tickets made a small tear in each ticket to avoid confusing it with an unused one. As the number of books on the swap shelves dwindled, Gayla had a student replenish the supply. She tried to distribute the books in as equitable a fashion as possible during the week of the ticket redemption. This enabled students who did not come to the library until later in the week to still enjoy a variety of paperbacks from which to choose. At the end of the week 392 of the 786 books had been claimed. During the next two weeks all students were given the opportunity to claim any remaining book on the swap shelves with either an unused ticket or 10 cents. When Gayla brought the program to a close, sixty-three books remained on the cart. The basketball coach took these books to the local public library where he served on the Booksale Committee of the Friends' Group. Gayla got $32.40 out of the program which although not a great deal, was satisfactory since the primary objective of the program was to get students to read for pleasure, not to raise money.

Following the program, Gayla did two things. First, she wrote a formal summary report reflecting the participation figures and noting the amount of money generated. Then she prepared a more informal account as a news release and sent it to the student newspaper and the local newspaper. Along with the release sent to the local paper, she included a black and white photograph of a crowd of students selecting their books from the swap shelves. The local paper carried not only her story but the picture as well on the first page of the second section. At school she noticed students in the hallways carrying books which came from the swap program. She spent the $32.40 on a photo-essay book about the city where her high school was located. The book was displayed with a small card describing the history of its acquisition for a couple of weeks before it was added to the circulating collection.

"Senatorial Teleconferencing"

Since it was an election year, John Fairdale, the librarian at Rosedale High School, wanted to plan a program that would focus on the political process and relate directly to the government class required of all seniors. His thoughts kept returning to Sarah K. Penson, the first woman to represent the state in the U.S. Senate. Discussions with the political science faculty about the various possibilities elicited general enthusiasm and some helpful suggestions. Jerri Dore, the lead government teacher suggested the program would offer an opportunity to emphasize the importance of registering to vote since many of the senior students were approaching or had already reached the legal voting age.

Because Senator Penson's participation would provide the central focus for his program, John began with efforts to contact her or someone on her staff. A member of her office staff, contacted by phone, listened to John's explanation of his idea — to have the senator address the government students and then participate in a question and answer session directly from her office in Washington, D.C. in a "Senatorial Teleconference." (Earlier investigation had revealed that Senator Penson would not be back in her home state for the next two months.) About three days later, John received confirmation of the date and time Senator Penson would participate in the teleconferencing program. He prepared a final outline of the program, which he submitted, along with a cover memo, to his principal for official approval. Earlier the principal had verbally supported the idea, but both decided it would be better to obtain a confirmation from the senator before preparing extensive written descriptions of all the other necessary plans.

While the senator's teleconference with the students would constitute the focal point of the program, John planned to include additional components. To familiarize the students with Sarah Penson, he prepared a biographical sketch drawn from some of the library's political science reference books and the local newspapers. Additionally, a call to Senator Penson's local office produced a current photograph and multiple copies of general information booklets. A quick check of the community resource file provided the phone number of the local chapter of the League of Women Voters, as well as the names of several league members who gave presentations on the importance of participating in the political process through voting and how to register to vote. John then contacted the telephone company's local office to determine the equipment required to set up the conference call. A customer service representative assisted in determining exactly what equipment was needed and the cost involved. John planned to use a 150-seat teaching arena where a phone was already installed. The room had very good acoustics, comfortable seating, and provisions for using any audiovisual equipment a program might require. Both John and the service representative agreed that two amplification speakers and three audience participation microphones would produce a satisfactory arrangement. The service representative arranged for the equipment to be delivered and set up a day prior to the actual program. This would allow John to check all the instructions for proper operations and verify that everything worked properly while the service personnel were on the site.

With all the outside arrangements and costs confirmed, he outlined and submitted the memo in figure 16 to his principal for written approval.

To: Sherry Johnson

From: John Fairdale

Following our conversation regarding a teleconference program for senior government students I am submitting the following program outline for your approval:

I. Objectives

    A. To enrich understanding of and promote interest in our federal system of government.

    B. To encourage and emphasize the importance of voting as a way of participating in a democratic government.

    C. To provide direct contact with an elected member of the U.S. Senate.

II. Procedures/Methods

    A. Audiovisual presentation to provide biographical information on Senator Penson.

(Figure 16 continues on page 87.)

B. Lesson on the senatorial election process and the duties and responsibilities of a U.S. senator — coordinated by Jerri Dore and taught in a government class prior to the teleconference.

C. Telephone conference with Senator Sarah Penson.

D. Information on how to register to vote, provided by the local chapter of the League of Women Voters and available in the library for at least one week following the teleconference. (Note: If it meets with your approval, the League of Women Voters will provide personnel for four hours each day to explain the registration process. The league does not in any way endorse or represent any one political party or political philosophy. Let me know how you feel about their presence in the library.)

cc: Jerri Dore, Lead Teacher for Government

Fig. 16. Memorandum on teleconference program.

John received approval from the principal and arranged to join Jerri and the other two government teachers at the next curriculum meeting. The teachers planned the program lesson and included a description of what would happen during the teleconference program. They also arranged for the class of students which normally met in the afternoon to come to the teleconference, which would take place in the morning. Additionally, all agreed that some questions for the senator should be discussed with each class and students who would pose the questions designated in advance. If time permitted, students would be allowed to ask other questions as well.

The telephone equipment arrived and the installation completed as planned. Using another phone within the building they tested the teleconferencing equipment and made a slight adjustment to the volume on the speakers. A test of each of the microphones indicated they worked well. The classroom preparation lessons went well with several students eager to ask the senator questions. The short biographical audiovisual presentation about Senator Penson provided a frame of reference for the students as well as a visual image of her on the other end of the phone line.

On the day of the teleconference, John placed the call before an audience in the special teaching auditorium. Using one of the microphones, he introduced himself and the audience to Senator Penson, described briefly the background information already provided to the students, then turned the floor over to the senator. Senator Penson proved to be an excellent speaker, expressing her delight in the students' interest in the workings of the Senate and the election process. She described her specific committee assignments and other activities. Her presentation lasted about fifteen minutes. Then she asked for questions from the student audience. Students took their places at the microphones, introduced themselves and the question and answer session began. At the end of another fifteen minutes, John thanked the senator for her time and interest in participating in the program. The students in a group said their good-byes and gave Senator Penson a warm round of applause.

After breaking the phone connection, Jerri opened the floor for additional discussion. The fact that the students still had many unasked questions quickly became apparent. Jerri encouraged students to visit members of the local chapter of the League of Women Voters who would be in the library during the following week to provide additional information on the election process and directions for registering to vote. Additionally, John had arranged a display of library materials relating to the political process and government (at all jurisdictional levels) located near the table where the voting information was available.

The following week there was much activity in this area of the library. Students came by for voting information and at the end of each day John found himself rearranging the political science display which the students had obviously examined. Each class wrote Senator Penson a letter expressing their thanks for her interest and participation in the program. Jerri collected these letters and passed them on to John who added his own word of thanks before mailing them to the senator. Additionally, he wrote a letter of appreciation to the League of Women Voters and a memo of thanks to the government faculty for their support and assistance.

The expense for the call (equipment and long-distance charges) amounted to $75. When the principal described the program to the local parent support group it readily agreed to cover the cost from its budget (she had expected to cover the costs from the school budget). Several weeks later, an illustrated book on Washington, D.C. arrived in the library mail with the inscription "To all the 'now-and-future' voters of Rosedale High — Exercise your right and privilege — it was a pleasure to visit with you! Senator Sarah K. Penson." After showing the book to the principal and the government faculty, John added it to the library's new books display. In its next issue, the student newspaper featured an article about the teleconference.

"Exploring Space"

"Dull and boring!" High school librarian Julie Casey often heard or overheard incoming freshmen students at Chaymore Senior High refer to library orientation as "dull and boring." Julie intended to try her best to find a better way to provide library orientation. While pondering this problem, she remembered the success of her library program the previous year which featured the school clubs and related library resource center material and equipment. She decided to try turning orientation into a program format centered around a theme that would add interest while still accomplishing the primary objectives of library orientation—introducing the major features of the library and its resources to the freshmen. After further consideration, she selected "Exploring Space" as her central theme.

"Exploring space in the library": an exhibit on loan from NASA.

The English department handled the scheduling of student participation because the English teachers were responsible for bringing the freshman class to the library at the beginning of each fall semester, usually during the third or fourth week of school. The program would begin in the library's large teaching classroom. Instead of the standard lecture with handouts, Julie arranged to borrow the film, "Houston, We've Got a Problem," from NASA. This film told the story of how, after an explosion during the Apollo 13 mission, the lives of all the crew were saved by some innovative and quick work on the part of specialists on Earth working in concert with crew. The film, designed to be the attention-grabber, proved successful. The success of the remainder of the orientation program required a great deal of creativity on Julie's part.

Her first step consisted of listing all the essential elements she needed to cover. It included such things as the location of the various essential components of the library—reference collection, card catalog, pamphlet file, community resource file, microfilm and microfilm reader/copiers. Next she defined just exactly how much information she wished to cover with the students and the method she would use to present it. She hoped to somehow carry through the space exploration theme.

For each of the components to be covered Julie prepared a short script covering all the information essential to understanding that particular area. Then she transcribed each script onto a separate tape. Julie enlisted some additional help in order to vary the voices heard at what would become an information station. Using a tape player and multi-unit head sets Julie arranged the stations to accommodate fifteen students. She then prepared a color coded library map identifying each of the library components covered in the orientation. The art and science departments provided large signs (color coded to match the map) to be suspended over each information station along with space related exhibits such as posters and models.

To ensure a relatively smooth traffic flow, each station was numbered, with the numbers included on the map and suspended sign. Following the film presentation, Julie divided the students into groups no larger than fifteen and assigned a station number where the exploration process would begin. She instructed the students to proceed to the assigned area, put on the head sets, and press "play," which was clearly marked on the tape machine. Julie also requested that someone in the group press the rewind button (also clearly marked). Then the group would proceed to the next station following the numerical order. She urged the students to keep the maps for future reference when returning to the library to fulfill the various assignments during the year.

In keeping with the theme of space exploration, the library staff dressed in inexpensive blue jump suits with space patches from a local souvenir shop. They added their names above the breast pocket in large yellow letters, which provided the students with visual name-face identification of the library staff. Julie hoped this would make students more comfortable in seeking help during return visits to the library.

The program went well. The film served its purpose and the groups moved from station to station smoothly. One tape player refused to work, but it was quickly replaced with a spare which had been set aside expressly for that purpose. When the orientation had been completed, Julie wrote an organized description of the program to be stored with the tapes, map master copy, and jump suits for future use. She left the station signs in place for six weeks to help students as they returned to use the library. Finally she prepared a brief fact-gathering sheet for the teachers whose classes had participated in this new style of orientation. She included specific questions as to how the program might be improved and asked for general reaction (including comments students might have made after returning to the classroom). A closing note, Julie and her staff noticed after the program that many of the freshmen they passed in the hall or encountered in the cafeteria recognized them.

5

After the Program Is Over
Follow-up and Evaluation

The program is over; what now? First, breathe a sigh of satisfaction and/or relief. However, before much time elapses, there are wrap-up activities which must be taken care of in order to bring a polished closure to the project. One of these activities involves the simple courtesy of expressing appreciation and saying thank you to the participants. Additionally the resource file will need to be updated, data collected for use in evaluation of the program, and a summary of the event compiled for inclusion in the annual report.

The extent and complexity of the follow-up or postprogram activities which are described in this chapter is generally in direct proportion to the size and complexity of the program itself. Integrate the ground work for the follow-up activities in the planning stages of your program and they will proceed much more smoothly and not require as much time and effort. However, regardless of whether or not the follow-up activities were included in the planning process, a program is not finished until they have been performed. A number of forms included in this chapter may prove useful in completing the various follow-up tasks. These forms may be tailored to meet specific needs, circumstances, or individual situations.

SAYING THANK-YOU

The cardinal rule for thank-yous is **Do Not Postpone Them**. This postprogram activity must be done immediately. Some types of thank-yous lend themselves to preprogram completion. One example would be preparation of certificates of appreciation from the library for participants in the program. The type of thank-you or acknowledgment employed depends on the nature of the action that triggers it. Use a formal, typed thank-you when an individual, group, or company has made a significant contribution to the program. If an individual has donated time and/or material on behalf of an institution, business, or organization, send a copy of the acknowledgment of appreciation to that individual's supervisor or company president.

For parents, community volunteers, or any participants in this general category, an informal handwritten note of thanks in more personal language may be preferred. If teachers or other school staff have lent a helping hand, their efforts merit a written acknowledgment as well. An interoffice memo may be chosen as long as a written form of some type is used. Although it is appropriate to reinforce appreciation verbally, do not use this as a substitute for the written thank-you.

One final point, often the benefactors of the programming—students and/or teachers—should also acknowledge their appreciation. Students can write notes, letters, a group letter (perhaps as part of a language lesson), or draw pictures or send a verbal message using audio tape recordings. Encourage these kinds of activities and assist the teachers by offering to take the responsibility for delivering the messages of appreciation to the appropriate recipient.

UPDATING THE RESOURCE FILE

Although chapter 3 details the procedure for a regular maintenance of the community resource file, an update of any file used in a specific program should be done after the program. After the event is over, pull any file used and add, remove, or change any pertinent information:

1. Record the use of resources (date, time, method, etc.).

2. Correct any information that has changed such as names, addresses, and phone numbers used in making contacts and arrangements.

3. Update policy information relating to resources, noting changes in fees (or addition of fees to formerly free services). Add any new features that have been discovered during the program you have just completed.

4. Briefly include any feedback received on the performance of guests. Note both negative as well as positive reactions.

5. Add new files as new resources are discovered. This can be done at any time, but often programming prompts the discovery of new sources for entries.

6. Delete files for resources which have become obsolete. Many phenomena affect the usefulness of the information in the file — people move, companies merge or close. When the source is no longer viable, throw the folder away.

Do not substitute this follow-up maintenance of the community resource file for regular updating as described in chapter 3. Use the preceding checklist for postprogramming work on the file. If there simply is not enough time to enter or delete information following a program, an alternate plan must be chosen in order to avoid the loss of vital information.

One alternate plan involves setting up a separate place for information on additions, changes, or deletions to the resource file. For example, at the beginning of the file include a folder labeled "Resource file update information." Or keep a folder of this type in your desk for convenience, remembering you alone have access to it. Store all information, regardless of the resource to which it relates, in this file. Soon a virtual myriad of material — notes on cards, brochures, lists — will accumulate and the folder will be bulging. Exercise some discipline and sort the file contents in a fashion depending upon the action required in order to update the resource file. Then proceed to make the necessary changes. Perhaps a student assistant or parent volunteer can make some or most of the corrections. The essential point remains unchanged: take time to update.

TEACHER EVALUATIONS

Immediately following a program, actively seek feedback from the teaching staff and administrative staff, if appropriate, while they have a clear memory of all that has happened. Written responses provide a far more valid and accurate source of evaluation. (For a sample evaluation form, see figure 14, page 77.) When preparing to gather written evaluation, keep the following points in mind.

1. Timely gathering of feedback provides the most accurate data as respondents will have clear memories of all the program events.

2. Use as simple an instrument as possible for the purpose of data collection. Design or select the form with ease of completion in mind.

3. Structure your questions carefully and precisely. Do not use vague generalities. For example, "Students were attentive to the speaker" ____ high degree ____ moderately ____ not at all is better than "The students like the speaker" ____ Yes ____ No.

4. In a timely fashion actively collect the responses rather than waiting for them to be returned.

5. Protect the anonymity of each person completing a form.

In some cases the evaluations for various segments of a program should be analyzed as well as the program as a whole. A little planning of the design of the evaluation form allows the librarian such an analysis without a great deal of extra work. Use figure 14, page 77, for an example as a springboard for your own design.

Provide space for open-ended comments and/or suggestions. Remember responses to such questions require more time to complete, and therefore may elicit no response or only a vague answer which is difficult to quantify. Do not defeat the purpose of evaluation by using a poorly designed questionnaire with vaguely worded questions. Additionally, keep a log or notes of some sort for recording informal feedback, which may be received in places such as the office, hallway, the cafeteria, or the school parking lot. Do not trust this oral feedback to memory. Also remember it carries a built-in positive bias, as few will volunteer to criticize someone to their face.

STUDENT EVALUATIONS

Student evaluations of a program will provide equally important information. Consider the age of the students involved and the nature of the program when planning how to gather student feedback. As with faculty, gather both formal and informal reactions. Although methods similar to those used with faculty may be employed, don't overlook some nontraditional sources for data as well. For example, if photographs or a video tape of the program activities are available, examine the audience and the audience response (or lack thereof) as recorded on any visual or audio reproduction. Study the faces, listen to the sounds. This type of analysis, if done objectively, will provide some valuable information about how the audience responded to the program.

Along more conventional lines, gather data using student response forms (figures 17, page 98 and 18, page 99). Use the same guidelines for student response forms as with faculty evaluations. Questions on the forms should be clear and specific. The forms themselves should require minimum time and effort on the part of the student. Structure the questions carefully so that the responses will truly reflect the students' reaction to the program. Plan the format in such a way that tabulation of the responses proceeds quickly and each respondent can remain anonymous if desired. Provide for open-ended comments, criticisms, and observations, but don't depend on it for the core of your student evaluation results.

(Text continues on page 100.)

LIBRARY PROGRAM

Circle the face that shows how you feel.

1. I liked the program.

2. I hope we have another library program.

3. I want to take a library book home this week.

Fig. 17. Sample program evaluation form for students (K-2nd grades).

WE WANT YOUR OPINION, PLEASE!

MEETING OUR LOCAL AUTHORS
(LRC Special Program)

1. I liked hearing what the authors told us.   Yes _____   No _____

2. I have read at least one of the authors' books.   Yes _____   No _____

3. I want to read at least one of the books in the library display.   Yes _____   No _____

4. I could hear what the authors said.   Yes _____   No _____

5. I could see the speakers and video monitor easily.   Yes _____   No _____

6. I hope we have another special program in the LRC.   Yes _____   No _____

I thought the best part of the program was:

The part of the program I liked least was:

Could we have a program about:

PLEASE GIVE THIS FORM TO YOUR TEACHER. SHE WILL SEND IT TO ME IN THE LRC.

Marcy Carrington,
LRC

Fig. 18. Sample program evaluation form for students.

LIBRARY STATISTICS

In addition to the data gathered which is directly related to the evaluation of a specific library program, survey the general library statistics immediately following a program. Consider all of the data which is routinely collected and recorded. Significant changes in library statistics immediately following a program provide additional information in program evaluation. If no changes are detected after a program in the library as a whole, data which address the effects of the program on particular aspects of library usage are still available. Consider briefly the various types of statistics generally kept and their potential relationship to library programming (see figure 19).

Circulation

Library statistics usually brings to mind circulation counts: the number of books, magazines, tapes, etc., that are checked out to users. Additionally, the type of user — students, teachers, or staff — checking out the various items may also be recorded. Programming can affect a rise in circulation in general, or more specifically, a rise in the circulation of certain parts of the library's collection. If circulation records are not kept by class number, consider doing so at least for a period of several weeks following the program. Then take a sample long after the program is over to provide a basis for comparison. This assumes, of course, that at least one objective of the program was to promote an increased use of the library, either the collection in general or a certain portion of the library's materials. Of a more general nature, but equally appropriate, are comparisons of circulation data for periods of time surrounding library programming and data from periods of times there has been little or no programming.

Usage

Librarians have devised numerous methods for monitoring and recording patron usage of the facilities. Some count each person or user who enters the library, while other school librarians record the number of classes that visit the library on a daily, weekly, or biweekly basis. The latter method is particularly prevalent in the public school setting. The sample census count provides yet another way of monitoring activity in the library. Programming should not affect the normal routine for recording library usage, unless this kind of data is not currently recorded. If some method of monitoring usage is not in place, this procedure must be incorporated into

LIBRARY PROGRAM STATISTICS

1. Number of students participating in the _____ program

2. Student response to the program:

   Liked _____   No opinion _____

   Disliked _____

3. Average weekly circulation prior to pro-   _____ gram (previous 8 weeks)

4. Average weekly circulation following the   _____ program (for 8 weeks)

5. Number of classes invited to participate   _____

   Number of classes actually participating   _____

6. Teacher response to the program:

   Favorable _____   No opinion _____

   Unfavorable _____

7. Number of publicity notices appearing   _____ through local media

8. Number of parent comments (favorable)   _____

   Number of parent comments (unfavorable)   _____

Miscellaneous notes:

Fig. 19. Sample form for statistical data.

the daily activities prior to presenting any special programs. This will establish a basis of normal or average library usage.

Once data reflecting average library usage has been recorded on a regular basis, observe what happens to this data following the initialization of programming activities. Regardless of whether increasing library use is one of the program objectives, note if this phenomenon occurs. If you are rusty on the statistical analysis formulas, pull out the text on educational statistics. Better still, if the library has a microcomputer, let the computer do the work. Use the machine to store and analyze the data, and provide a printed report or even computer-generated graphics reflecting the results. If possible enlist a student from the school computer club to enter the data. Keeping consistent records on usage will provide additional feedback on the value and impact of library programming. Additionally, this information can be included in summary reports, annual reports, or in what ever type of report the school requires. The information also could be submitted to a parent newsletter or school newspaper.

ANALYZING THE DATA

After spending valuable time collecting and recording the various types of data relating to the program, an analysis of this information should provide the logical conclusion to the process. Realize that many different levels of analysis exist. For those who excel in the verbal rather than quantitative skills, just the word analysis can cause a slight chill. If the reverse is true, skim or skip the next few paragraphs.

One of the simpler forms of data analysis is a data summary which provides insights into what happens in the library over extended periods of time. Weekly, monthly, semiannual, and annual summaries are all of value. Simple bar graphs prepared on an annual basis, for example, clearly show patterns of circulation or use as illustrated in figure 20. These visual representations of data fit nicely into annual reports or as enlargements posted on the library bulletin board and may attract interest from teachers, students, and administrators.

Comparisons of usage or circulation data collected during nonprogramming periods may provide further insight on the effect or value of programming. Take into consideration the feedback you receive on the program. It would be expected that a program which received positive evaluations should generate a rise both in circulation and usage, while poorly received programs should not cause any increase in library statistics. Keep in mind, the key words are expect and should. Data analysis either confirms or negates expectations.

A mathematically sound statistical analysis involves the application of detailed analysis using such methods as standard deviation, analysis of

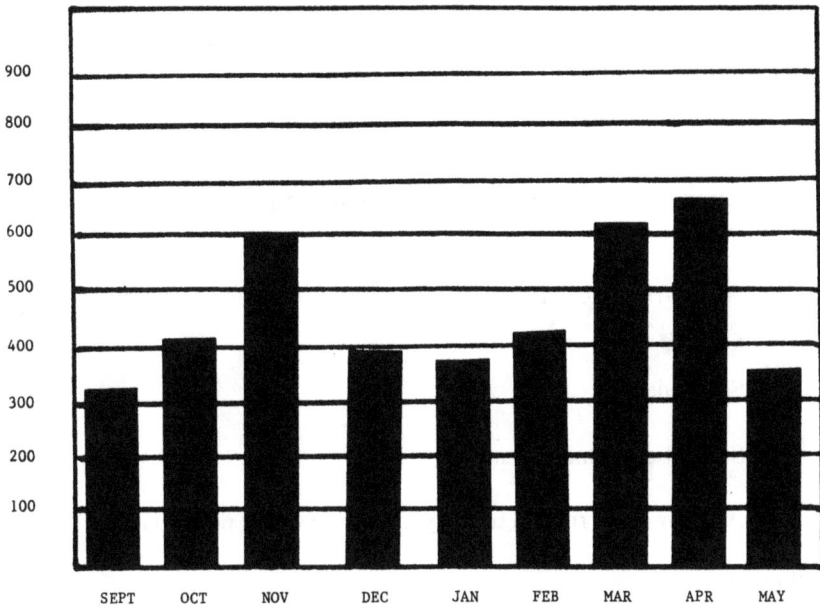

Fig. 20. Circulation 1984/85.

variance, or chi-square. However, the majority of librarians do not possess these highly technical skills and would find such analysis beyond their means. Regardless of whether a general survey type analysis or detailed application of statistical formulas is chosen, interpretation of the data will provide useful insights and understandings of the effect or lack of effect of programming on library usage.

REPORTS AND RECORDS

The preceding sections of this chapter provide much of the information needed to keep good records and prepare appropriate reports. At this point it is useful to reiterate and elaborate on this topic.

Establish a file for each program in order to have a place to put every scrap of paper, note, letter, list, etc., that accumulates. File all formal information—copies of letters sent, the memo of approval from the principal—in this file as well. As time permits, add this miscellaneous data to thè appropriate list, planning document or permanent folder in the community resource file. Following the program, discard any information in this folder that is no longer needed and add items that have accumulated such as individual evaluation forms. The following list includes the kinds of information typically kept in a program file.

- General outline of the program.

- Copies of all memos or written correspondence relating to the program.

- Any written clearance required by the administration or district policy.

- Schedules.

- Special equipment needs.

- Anything else related to the program that you need to locate quickly.

When in doubt, **file it**.

Summary and Annual Reports

This program file provides easy access to all the data and information needed to write a summary report covering the entire program. It brings some ordered closure to all the activity related to the program as a whole. Share the summary, including the evaluation and feedback data with the principal and any others who would benefit from the report or appreciate the information it contains. The report might even provide additional leverage when preparing next year's budget request.

At the end of the year when preparing the annual report, simply append a copy of the final summary report for each of that year's special programs. If this is inappropriate, use the summary report to prepare a synopsis of what occurred to be included in the annual report. Once again, the intricacy and extent of the program will determine the length and complexity of these reports.

EXTENDED INFLUENCES

Following the completion of a program, data collection and analysis, and compilation of some type of summary report, return to a normal routine and watch for ripple effects or after shocks. Consider the program as a rock tossed into the center of a quiet pond and observe the concentric rings, or effects of the library program, spread beyond the initial objectives. Some of the effects caused by the program, may never surface while others may eventually be seen.

For example, enthusiastic responses expressed to a parent will go officially unrecorded unless the parent has an occasion to mention the comments to the librarian. However, the parent may comment on the student's excitement to other parents in the neighborhood, thus reinforcing positive feelings about the school library and the librarian's role in the educational process. Eventually these positive attitudes may generate some concrete results such as additional support for library needs from the school's parent's organization. However, the librarian will never be able to validate these kinds of extended impacts that programming may generate.

If the program attracts interest from the local media in the form of newspaper stories, radio announcements, or television coverage, the school as well as the library will enjoy positive recognition in the community. Students enjoying special educational activities in the school library can offer a refreshing alternative on the 6:00 news. Although the librarian can verify the coverage occurred, the community reaction cannot be assessed. Perhaps positive media coverage will contribute toward favorable voter response to school taxes. Regardless of the identifiable results, press coverage is welcomed at any time.

Consider also the impact of the program on those who presented it or in some way participated in the preparation. If community members or community businesses contributed to the activities, they will experience some postprogramming effects. Listed below are some possible reactions from participants:

- Gain a new respect for the quality of education in the community.

- Promote additional support for future requests for special programming.

- Promote communication between the professional educators and other elements within the community.

Any one of these possibilities or the countless others constitute a significant impact resulting from the initial programming efforts.

Another facet of extended influence relates to the students. Some of their immediate reactions to the program have been measured during the evaluation process. However, the students' feelings or attitudes about the library and its services may change in a positive way and affect their entire future relationship with libraries. Students may feel more at ease in the library and may better understand its arrangement. This may generate more efficient and frequent use of all library materials. Perhaps some students will no longer feel embarrassed to ask for help now that they recognize the librarian and feel comfortable expressing their needs. Again, these kinds of influences of programming may never be objectively documented, but they do occur.

None of what has been described will transpire unless the first step is taken. Incorporate programming into the regular activities of library operations **now**. Begin the planning process without delay and see it through. It is an exciting and worthwhile experience.

Appendix A
Library Program Plan

Topic: Treasure Hunting

Target Group: Fifth Grade

Time: 45 minutes

Location: Library

Objectives:

1. Students will gain knowledge from guest speakers concerning the equipment used in treasure hunting.

2. Students will become familiar with the famous treasures which have been discovered throughout the world.

3. Students will become acquainted with available library materials on the topic.

Materials:

Filmstrip
Slide show
Treasure maps
Book displays
Posters
Guest speakers

Procedures:

1. Introduce the topic with a filmstrip.

2. Two guest speakers—both amateur treasure hunters—will show slides and speak to the students about the topic.

3. The speakers will end the session with a 10-minute question-and-answer period.

Follow-up Activities:

1. Filmstrips and books on the topic will be made available to teachers.

2. The learning center area of the library will focus upon the topic. A filmstrip on the topic will be available in one center. A second center will include a treasure-hunting game. In the third center, students will enjoy a crossword puzzle. The fourth center will focus on reference materials on the subject.

3. Reference materials concerning the topic will be highlighted in the library. Teachers will be encouraged to assign reference activities on the topic.

Follow-up Correspondence:

1. The students will be encouraged to send thank-you notes to the guests.

2. The librarian will send a letter of appreciation to the guests.

Evaluation of the Program:

1. Circulation rate increase

2. Informal student comments

3. Circulation of books on display

4. Formal questionnaire to teachers

5. Learning center usage

Appendix B
Selective Topical
Bibliography

GENERAL SOURCES

Aaron, Shirley L. "School/Public Library Cooperation: A State of the Art Review." Syracuse, N.Y.: ERIC Clearinghouse on Information Resources, 1980. (ED 192 810).

Angus, Beatrice E. "Appraisal of the New York State School Library System." Syracuse, N.Y.: ERIC Clearinghouse on Information Resources, 1980. (ED 220 099).

Blazek, Ronald. *Influencing Students Toward Media Center Use: An Experimental Investigation in Mathematics*. Chicago: American Library Association, 1975.

Carpenter, Ray L., and Ellen Storey Vasu. *Statistical Methods for Librarians*. Chicago: American Library Association, 1978.

Hodges, Yvonne A., Judy Gray, and William J. Reeves. "High School Students' Attitudes Towards the Media Program—What Makes the Difference?" Syracuse, N.Y.: ERIC Clearinghouse on Information Resources, 1982. (ED 223 221).

Schon, Isabel, et al. "The Effects of a Special Library Program on Elementary Students' Library Use and Attitudes." *School Library Media Quarterly* 12 (Spring 1984): 227-31.

School Library Media Annual. Shirley L. Aaron and Pat R. Scales, eds. Littleton, Colo.: Libraries Unlimited, 1983- .

Steinaker, Norman. "Ten Years Hence: The Curriculum Development and Usage Center." *Educational Leadership* 33 (March 1976): 447-49.

Swisher, Robert, and Charles McClure. *Research for Decision Making: Methods for Librarians*. Chicago: American Library Association, 1984.

Young, Robert K., and Donald J. Veldman. *Introductory Statistics for the Behavioral Sciences*. 4th ed. New York: Holt, Rinehart and Winston, 1981.

ADOLESCENT AND CHILDREN'S LITERATURE

Hopkins, Lee Bennett. "Book Sharing: Poetry Roundup-1985." *School Library Media Quarterly* 14 (Spring 1986): 144-45.

Koontz, Carol L., ed. *Connections: Using Contemporary Children's Literature (K-9) in the Classroom*. Urbana, Ill.: National Council of Teachers of English, 1986.

Leonard, Charlotte. *Tied Together: Topics and Thoughts for Introducing Children's Books*. Metuchen, N.J.: Scarecrow, 1980.

Moore, Vardina. *The Pleasure of Poetry with and by Children: A Handbook*. Metuchen, N.J.: Scarecrow, 1981.

Norton, Donna E. *Through the Eyes of a Child*. Columbus, Ohio: Charles E. Merrill, 1983.

Sullivan, Emilie P. *Beginning with Books*. Hingham, Mass.: Teaching Resources, 1980.

Sutherland, Zena, Mayhill Arbuthnot, and Dianne L. Monson. *Children and Books*. 7th ed. Glenview, Ill.: Scott, Foresman, 1980.

BULLETIN BOARDS, DISPLAYS, AND EXHIBITS

Bowers, Melvyn K. *Easy Bulletin Boards for the School Library*. Metuchen, N.J.: Scarecrow, 1974.

Bullough, Robert V. *Display Boards*. Englewood Cliffs, N.J.: Educational Technology Publications, 1980.

Canoles, Marian L. *The Creative Copycat II*. Littleton, Colo.: Libraries Unlimited, 1985.

Coplan, Kate. *How to Prepare and Promote Good Displays*. Dobbs Ferry, N.Y.: Oceana, 1974.

Coplan, Kate, and Constance Rosenthal. *Guide to Better Bulletin Boards: Time and Labor Saving Ideas for Teachers and Librarians*. Dobbs Ferry, N.Y.: Oceana, 1970.

Garvey, Mona. *Library Displays: Their Purpose, Construction, and Use*. New York: H. W. Wilson, 1969.

Heath, Alan. *Off the Wall: The Art of Book Display*. Littleton, Colo.: Libraries Unlimited, 1987.

Kohn, Rita. *Experiencing Displays*. Metuchen, N.J.: Scarecrow, 1982.

Posters. New York: Children's Book Council, 1981.

Wallick, Clair. *Looking for Ideas: A Display Manual for Libraries and Bookstores*. Metuchen, N.J.: Scarecrow, 1970.

COMMUNITY RESOURCES

Baptiste, H. Prentice, and Patricia J. Wilson. "Role of the School Librarian in Multicultural Education." *Catholic Library World* 57 (November/December 1985): 122-24.

Brown, James, Richard B. Lewis, and Fred Harcleroad. *AV Instruction: Technology, Media and Methods*. 6th ed. New York: McGraw-Hill, 1983.

Casciero, Albert J., and Raymond G. Roney. *Introduction to AV for Technical Assistants*. Littleton, Colo.: Libraries Unlimited, 1981.

Community Resources File in the Learning Center. Austin, Tex.: Texas Education Agency, Division of Instructional Resources, n.d.

Kimzey, Ann, Patricia J. Wilson, and Linda Garner. "Programming in the School Library with Community Resources." *Top of the News* 41 (Fall 1984): 89-92.

Libraries, Center for Children's Needs: Developing a Community Information File. Chicago: Association for Library Service to Children, American Library Association, 1974.

Lyngheim, Linda. "Build a State and Local History Collection." *School Library Journal* 33 (October 1986): 51.

Smallwood, Carol. *A Guide to Selected Agency Programs and Publications for Librarians and Teachers*. Littleton, Colo.: Libraries Unlimited, 1986.

Wood, Rulon Kent. *Community Resources*. Englewood Cliffs, N.J.: Educational Technology Publications, 1980.

Zelmer, A. C. Lynn. *Community Media Handbook*. 2nd ed. Metuchen, N.J.: Scarecrow, 1979.

LEARNING CENTERS

Beach, Don M. *Reaching Teenagers: Learning Centers for the Secondary Classroom*. Santa Monica, Calif.: Goodyear Publishing, 1977.

Davidson, Tom, et al. *The Learning Center Book: An Integrated Approach.* Pacific Palisades, Calif.: Goodyear Publishing, 1976.

Ducote, Richard L. *Learning Resource Center: Best of ERIC; A Selected, Annotated Bibliography.* Syracuse, N.Y.: ERIC Clearinghouse on Information Resources, 1977.

STORYTELLING, READING ALOUD, AND DRAMA

Anderson, Paul S. *Story Telling with the Flannel Board.* Minneapolis, Minn.: Denison, 1971.

Baker, Augusta, and Ellin Greene. *Storytelling: Art and Technique.* New York: R. R. Bowker, 1980.

Bauer, Caroline Feller. *Handbook for Storytellers.* Chicago: American Library Association, 1977.

Bodart, Joni. *Booktalk!* New York: H. W. Wilson, 1980.

Briggs, Nancy E., and Joseph A. Wagner. *Children's Literature through Storytelling and Drama.* Dubuque, Iowa: William C. Brown, 1979.

Champlin, Connie, and Nancy Renfro. *Storytelling with Puppets.* Chicago: American Library Association, 1985.

De Wit, Dorothy. *Children's Faces Looking Up: Program Building for the Storyteller.* Chicago: American Library Association, 1979.

Livo, Norma J., and Sandra A. Rietz. *Storytelling: Process and Practice.* Littleton, Colo.: Libraries Unlimited, 1986.

Livo, Norma J., and Sandra A. Rietz. *Storytelling Activities.* Littleton, Colo.: Libraries Unlimited, 1987.

Renfro, Nancy, and Ann Weiss Schwalb. "Show Centers for Library Media Centers: Establishing Puppet Performance Centers in the Library." *School Library Media Activities Monthly* 2 (January 1986): 29-36.

Ross, Ramon R. *Storyteller.* 2nd ed. Columbus, Ohio: Charles E. Merrill, 1980.

Sawyer, Ruth. *The Way of the Storyteller*. New York: Penguin, 1977.

Siks, Geraldine Brain. *Drama with Children*. 2nd ed. New York: Harper & Row, 1983.

Silverman, Eleanor. *Dramatics for Children*. Metuchen, N.J.: Scarecrow, 1983.

Simmen, René. *The World of Puppets*. New York: Crowell, 1975.

Sitarz, Paula Gaj. *Picture Book Story Hours: From Birthdays to Bears*. Littleton, Colo.: Libraries Unlimited, 1987.

Stahlschmidt, Agnes D., and Carol Schulte Johnson. "The Library Media Specialist and the Read-Aloud Program." *School Library Media Quarterly* 12 (Winter 1984): 146-49.

Stewig, John Warren. "Storyteller: Endangered Species?" *Language Arts* 55 (March 1978): 339-45.

Trelease, Jim. *The Read-Aloud Handbook*. New York: Penguin, 1985.

PROGRAMS FOR LIBRARIES

Baker, Philip D. *The Library Media Program and the School*. Littleton, Colo.: Libraries Unlimited, 1984.

Baker, Philip D. *School and Public Library Media Programs for Children and Young Adults*. Syracuse, N.Y.: Gaylord Professional Publications, 1976.

Carparelli, Felicia A., comp. *A Practical Approach to Programming*. Chicago: American Library Association, 1982.

Faculjak, Barbara A. "Library Theater Makes Books Come Alive!" *School Library Media Quarterly* 14 (Summer 1986): 180-81.

Greenblatt, Melinda. "Expanding Children's Programming in School and Public Libraries." *Wilson Library Bulletin* 54 (October 1979): 99-102.

Hackman, Mary H. *Library Media Skills and the Senior High School English Program*. Edited by Paula Kay Montgomery. Littleton, Colo.: Libraries Unlimited, 1985.

Haglund, Elaine J., and Marcia L. Harris. *On This Day: A Collection of Everyday Events and Activities for the Media Center, Library, and Classroom.* Littleton, Colo.: Libraries Unlimited, 1983.

Robotham, John S., and Lydia LaFleur. *Library Programs: How to Select, Plan and Produce Them.* 2nd ed. Metuchen, N.J.: Scarecrow, 1981.

Seaver, Alice R. *Library Media Skills: Strategies for Instructing Primary Students.* Edited by Paula Kay Montgomery. Littleton, Colo.: Libraries Unlimited, 1984.

Sherman, Louis. "Practically Speaking: Have a Story Lunch." *School Library Journal* 33 (October 1986): 120-21.

Silverman, Eleanor. *101 Media Center Ideas.* Metuchen, N.J.: Scarecrow, 1980.

Van Vliet, Lucille W. *Media Skills for Middle Schools: Strategies for Library Media Specialists and Teachers.* Edited by Paula Kay Montgomery. Littleton, Colo.: Libraries Unlimited, 1984.

Walker, H. Thomas, and Paula Kay Montgomery. *Teaching Library Media Skills: An Instructional Program for Elementary and Middle School Students.* 2nd ed. Littleton, Colo.: Libraries Unlimited, 1983.

Wilkens, Lea-Ruth. "A Bathtub in the School Library?" *Childhood Education* 57 (March/April 1981): 213-15.

Zlotnick, Barbara Bradley. *Ready for Reference: Media Skills for Intermediate Students.* Edited by Paula Kay Montgomery. Littleton, Colo.: Libraries Unlimited, 1984.

PUBLICITY AND PUBLIC RELATIONS

Cook, Donald H. "The School Newsletter: Effective K-12 Communicator." *School Library Media Quarterly* 14 (Spring 1986): 131-32.

Eastman, Ann Heidbreder, and Evelyn Shaevel, eds. *Great Promotion Ideas II: JCD Library Public Relations Award Winners and Notables.* Chicago: American Library Association, 1986.

Edsall, Marian S. *Library Promotion Handbook*. Phoenix, Ariz.: Oryx Press, 1980.

Keefe, Betty, et al. "High Touch: PR, Practical Approaches to Public Relations." *School Library Media Quarterly* 14 (Spring 1986): 128-30.

Kies, Cossette. *Projecting a Positive Image through Public Relations*. Chicago: American Association of School Librarians, American Library Association, 1978.

Kohn, Rita, and Krysta Tepper. *You Can Do It: A PR Manual for Librarians*. Metuchen, N.J.: Scarecrow, 1981.

Persuasive Public Relations for Libraries. Kathleen Kelly Rummel and Esther Perica, eds. Chicago: American Library Association, 1983.

Sherman, Steve. *ABC's of Library Promotion*. 2nd ed. Metuchen, N.J.: Scarecrow, 1980.

SELECTING PRINT
AND NONPRINT MATERIALS

Brown, Lucy. *Core Media Collection for Elementary Schools*. New York: R. R. Bowker, 1978.

Brown, Lucy. *Core Media Collection for Secondary Schools*. New York: R. R. Bowker, 1981.

Carlsen, G. Robert. *Books and the Teenage Reader: A Guide for Teachers, Librarians and Parents*. 2nd ed. New York: Harper & Row, 1980.

Carter, Yvonne B., and Barbara Spriestersbach. *Aids to Media Selection for Students and Teachers*. McFarland, Wis.: National Association of State Educational Media Professionals, 1985.

Gillespie, John T., and Christine B. Gilbert, eds. *Best Books for Children: Preschool through the Middle Grades*. 3rd ed. New York: R. R. Bowker, 1985.

Mahoney, Ellen, and Leah Wilcox. *Ready, Set, Read: Best Books to Prepare Preschoolers*. Metuchen, N.J.: Scarecrow, 1985.

A Multimedia Approach to Children's Literature. 3rd ed. Mary Alice Hunt, ed. Chicago: American Library Association, 1983.

National Council of Teachers of English. Committee on the Elementary School Booklist. *Adventuring with Books: A Booklist for Pre-K-Grade 6.* new ed. Dianne L. Monson, ed. Urbana, Ill.: National Council of Teachers of English, 1985.

Peterson, Carolyn, and Brenny Hall. *Story Programs: A Source Book of Materials.* Metuchen, N.J.: Scarecrow, 1980.

Richardson, Selma K. *Magazines for Children: A Guide for Parents, Teachers, and Librarians.* Chicago: American Library Association, 1983.

Richardson, Selma K. *Magazines for Young Adults: Selections for School and Public Libraries.* Chicago: American Library Association, 1984.

Sive, Mary. *Selecting Instructional Media: A Guide to Audiovisual and Other Instructional Media Lists.* 3rd ed. Littleton, Colo.: Libraries Unlimited, 1983.

Smallwood, Carol. *Exceptional Free Library Resource Materials.* Littleton, Colo.: Libraries Unlimited, 1984.

Sutherland, Zena. *The Best in Children's Books: The University of Chicago Guide to Children's Literature 1979-1984.* Chicago: University of Chicago Press, 1986.

The Video Source Book. 8th ed. Syosset, N.Y.: National Video Clearinghouse, 1986.

Woodbury, Marda. *Selecting Materials for Instruction: Media and the Curriculum.* Littleton, Colo.: Libraries Unlimited, 1980.

Wynar, Christine Gehrt. *Guide to Reference Books for School Media Centers.* 3rd ed. Littleton, Colo.: Libraries Unlimited, 1986.

TELECONFERENCING

Bunson, Stan. "Checklists for Teleconferencing Coordinators." *Tech Trends* 31 (May/June 1986): 30-32.

Parker, Lorne A., and Christine Olgren, comps. *Teleconferencing and Interactive Media*. Madison, Wis.: Center for Interactive Programs, Wisconsin University, 1980. (ED 194 045).

Scales, Pat. "Dial an Author: How to Develop a Successful Reader-Writer Interview Program." New York: Bantam Books, 1981.

VOLUNTEERS FOR LIBRARIES

Bennett, Linda Leveque. *Volunteers in the School Media Center*. Littleton, Colo.: Libraries Unlimited, 1984.

Hoagland, Mary Arthur. "Training and Gaining School Library Volunteers." *Catholic Library World* 56 (December 1984): 213-16.

Veele, Mary L. *The School Volunteer's Handbook*. Holmes Beach, Fla.: Learning Publications, 1977.

Index